# The Only Way Out

## The Real King Charles

ISBN: 978-0-692-16928-5

# DEDICATION

Trustee James H. Mortimer, III of the Mariners' Temple Baptist Church. The building is located at 3 Henry Street, New York, New York [10038.] Trustee James H. Mortimer, III A giant of a man with a strong but gentle reassuring voice of love.

# CONTENTS

This page was left blank intentionally

# ACKNOWLEDGMENTS

To my two daughters, Princess Ryane and Candyce Hecker, thank for spending countless hours proofreading and editing this Manual.

To my beautiful, super intelligent six year old daughter, Royelle Fehrlin, thank you for picking the color for the cover of this Manual.

To my sister Yasmine Hecker, thank for all of your help, sharing your honest opinion and helping to see this book to fruition.

To my website designer, Joseph Thompson, thank for designing my website, thank you for putting up with my demanding personality and thank you for having enough confidence in my knowledge of the system to use one of the techniques in this Manual to beat a fraudulent, criminal charge against you.

To my friend, Samuel White, Jr., thank you for teaching me sharpen by writing skills.

To my friend, Sophia Coffee, thank you for inspiring me to write.

This Page was left blank intentionally

## Disclaimer

The information contained in this **Powerful Manual** is for educational purposes only. There is nothing set forth herein intended to be legal advice nor shall it be construed as such. This **Powerful Manual** is private in its entirety and non-negotiable between the parties.

Herein accordance with the Constitution of the United States of America, the intent of the author is to share information with his fellow de jure American National People, as well as with anyone who wishes to become a government de jure American National.

# www.theonlywayout.net

# Preface

For the record, this **Powerful Manual** is based on the personal experiences and successful, lawful outcomes of the author, as a **government de jure American National**, acting with full, unimpaired rights and standing in the law. However, there is another government that is currently in charge of the nation, and it is called the **government de facto**. The **government de facto** neglected to inform the American people about the alternative to the **government de facto**, which is the **government de jure**. These two governments **co-exist.** "We the People" have a choice of two governments in this great country of ours. The **government de facto** is **not** the true and lawful government; the **government de jure** is the true and lawful government. The author of this **Powerful Manual** pledges his allegiance to the government de jure where he enjoys his **true freedom. "Oh, beautiful America,"** please read the definition of the two governments in the segments below.

[BLACK'S LAW DICTIONARY: SIXTH EDITION (p. 697, ST. PAUL, MINN. WEST PUBLISHING CO. 1990) recognizes two governments.]

a) ["**Government de facto**. A government of fact. A government, actually exercising power and control, as opposed to the true and lawful government; a government not established according to the constitution of the nation, or not lawfully entitled to recognition or supremacy, but which has nevertheless supplanted or displaced the government de jure. [The] government [de facto is] deemed unlawful, or deemed wrongful or unjust, which, nevertheless receives presently habitual obedience from the bulk of the community."]

b) ["**Government de jure**. A government of right; the true and lawful government; a government established according to the constitution of the nation, and [is] lawfully entitled to recognition and supremacy [in] the administration of the nation, but which is actually cut off from power or control. A government deemed lawful, or deemed rightful or just, which, nevertheless, has been supplanted or displaced; that is to say, which receives not presently (although it received formerly) habitual obedience from the bulk of the community."]

To date, the author has had successful lawful outcomes in a divorce court, in a tenant/landlord court, and in other legal matters - when appearing specially and not generally on behalf of the debtor, in the courtroom until the matters were resolved. Thanks to the illegal and unethical courtroom tactics of the Magistrates who violated their Fiduciary duty, as well as The Constitution of the United States of America and the Uniform Commercial Code, the author was motivated to research the inner workings of the government de facto court system and its history. The author is now sharing this information with the American people and the people of the World. The author **protected** himself as a government de jure American National and has never lost a case in any government de facto courtroom. The author has found **the only way to protect oneself** in every courtroom. The government de facto courts only have jurisdiction over debtors. Note: a debtor's name is mainly spelled with all capital letters, for example (**ROBERT JOHN DOE**)**,** or in upper lower case with a middle initial (**Robert J. Doe**)**,** or with initials (**R.J.D.**)**.** These ways of spelling any Natural Person's Name in the English Language is a corruption of the spelling. The names of all American Natural People are spelled in upper, lower case letters, for example: (**Robert John Doe**). Now, some courts are spelling the first and last name of the people in upper, lower case letters, for example: **(Robert Doe).** However, in the English Language, the first letter of a person, place or "**THING**" is capitalized and those courts are looking at people as a **THING/ A CORPORATION**. Please do not fall for the OKIE DOKE, because a **CORPORATION CAN ONLY DEAL WITH A CORPORATION**. This **Powerful Manual** is written to help free the American National People from bondage. Martin Luther King, Jr. said, "...Let freedom ring from the mighty mountains of New York..."

This publication is designed to provide alternative information about the two factual governments in regard to jurisdiction over person and over subject matter. It is the author's hope that the American people, and the people of the World, will wake up to a brighter tomorrow with the understanding that the truth shall set them free, by non-violent measures.

The author of this **Powerful Manual** is not giving legal advice to anyone. If legal advice is needed, the author suggests that the reader seek professional legal services. The author is just fulfilling his duty to his countrywomen and countrymen thereto lawfully equip them with the right information that they will need to protect themselves in any courtroom. **Article IV, Section 4, of the Constitution of the United States of America, which is located in this Powerful Manual, starting on page 64 states, "The United States Constitution shall guarantee to every State in this Union, a Republican form of government."** Please do not get this wrong - The Constitution is not referring to the **Republican and Democratic Parties**. The Constitution is referring to a **lawful Republican form of government** in which the majority of the people have power over the government politicians.

The author of this **Powerful Manual** has made every effort to provide accurate and up-to-date information at the time of this publication. The author accepts no responsibility for errors or changes in the codes or laws promulgated by the government de facto, in what is known as **prima facie** law. **Prima facie** means, if you believe that it is a law and treat it like it is the law, and then it shall become the law. **Prima facie** is defined in **[BLACK'S LAW DICTIONARY: SIXTH EDITION** (p. 1189, ST. PAUL, MINN. WEST PUBLISHING CO. 1990). **Prima facie** is "Lat. At first sight; on the first appearance; on the face of it; so far as can be judged from the first disclosure; presumably; a fact presumed to be true <u>unless disproved by some evidence to the contrary</u>."] **The Constitution of the United States of America is the proof and the evidence to the contrary, that shall prove the government de facto codes and laws are fraudulent and without merit.**

<u>The Constitution of the United State of America</u> is the supreme law of the land that gives the de jure American National People the right, the power, and the freedom to agree or disagree with any government de facto code or law that is not in line with <u>The Constitution of the United States of America</u>.

## INTRODUCTION TO THE MOST POWERFUL, EYE-OPENING MANUAL ON THE PLANET

This **Powerful Manual** is the most enlightening **handbook** on the planet and can help all of the American people navigate the court system successfully, as well as expose the deceptions of the government de facto. The information in this **Powerful Manual** is the turning point towards freedom for the American people. This **Powerful Manual** can help people encumbered by fraudulent debt, due to lack of knowledge; the deceit of the government de facto; and the greed of the money powers of the world, like **The Federal Reserve Bank**. This **Powerful Manual** was written to put an end to the gentrification of the <u>poor and middle class communities in America - **forever**</u>. The Uniform Commercial Code deals with global commerce. <u>**The UCC is the most powerful code on the planet that works**</u> and <u>the Constitution of the United States of America is the supreme law of the land in America that works</u>.

# The Only Way Out

1. For the record, this is the most **Powerful Manual** on the planet, and it will teach you, the reader, <u>**the correct way to enter into any courtroom and never lose your Rights, Money, Freedom, Property or Life**</u>. Whether you choose to use an Attorney to defend you, or if you try to represent yourself, you will be putting your Rights, Money, Freedom, Property and Life in jeopardy. This **Powerful Manual** is written to teach the readers how to correctly enter into any courtroom, protect themselves and never lose.

2. The author estimates that 98.5% of the American population acknowledges the government de facto as being the true and lawful government, which is far from the truth. The government de facto is not the true and lawful government, and the American people are not mandated to be citizens of the government de facto. The unlawful government de facto willfully neglected to inform the American people that they have a choice of two governments that **coexist,** in this great country of ours. <u>**Why is the government de facto hiding this information from the American people**</u>?

3. The author of this **Powerful Manual** is a government de jure American National, acting with full, unimpaired rights and standing in the law. The author is protected by The Constitution of the United States of America of 1787 in its full capacity and may be the only real creditor in every courtroom that he enters. If you are a government de facto citizen, you are a debtor with no power. However, if you choose to become a government de jure American National, you will be protected by the <u>Constitution of the United States of America</u>, and you too can be a creditor in every courtroom that you walk into. Please remember that all defendants are debtors.

4. The American people can stop being abused by the government de facto politicians who are voted into office. Most people are so brainwashed and blind, and cannot see the truth shining in front of their eyes. The Founding Fathers of America and the late President John Fitzgerald Kennedy must be turning over in their graves because, **"<u>We the People</u>,"** **let the corporate government de facto take control of the lives of the majority of the American People.**

5. The greatest thing about becoming a government de jure American National is that you shall lose nothing, but gain your freedom and much more. The government de jure American National People's Rights, Freedoms and Liberties cannot be taken away or denied. If you decide to become a government de jure American National, you must never violate anyone else's Constitutional Rights and you should conduct yourself in a civilized and respectable manner at all times. The penalties for Constitutional Rights violations can be very harsh.

## ENACTMENT OF CONSTITUTIONAL RIGHTS

1. The Constitution of the United States of America still has wings and can fly. The American people have been given Civil Rights. The American people lost their Constitutional Rights a long time ago, which is their ironclad, guaranteed right to freedom. Constitutional rights must be enacted, and if they are is not enacted, they shall be assumed waived. The information in this **Powerful Manual** shall help people preserve their Rights, Money, Freedom, Property and Lives. If **we the people** study and use this **Powerful Manual** correctly, freedom is not that far away!


2. If any police officer violates any of your Constitutional Rights, it is considered a Class-B Felony, and you can file a claim against the police officer(s) in the jurisdiction the violation occurred. The claim against the police officer can be for up to (One Million Dollars) $1,000,000. You may also be able to sue the City or Town for (One Million Dollars) $1,000,000. If a police officer is convicted of any Constitutional Rights violations, she or he can no longer be a police officer, and she or he may be imprisoned for a lengthy period of time. Please remember that you must enact your Constitutional Rights first, or they shall be assumed waived. To enact your Constitutional Rights, you must make this following statement to the police officers, medics, magistrates and to whomever else that may try to violate any of your Constitutional Rights: "**For the record, all rights are reserved, pertaining to The Constitution of the United States of America.**" It is that simple. If you do not enact your constitutional rights, a police officer can do almost anything she or he wants to do to you, with little or no repercussions. Note: Police officers do not know the law. They were only taught codes. Let's go back in time to the enactment of the Federal Reserve Act.

## THE FRAUD BEHIND THE FEDERAL RESERVE ACT

1. On December 23, 1913, the majority of Congress, who were opposed to the Federal Reserve Act bill, was already on Christmas vacation. Hence, the Federal Reserve Act bill passed, and **President Wilson** quickly signed that bill into law on the same day of the bill passing. The author of this manual saw a program on WNET, Public Broadcasting Service Channel 13, that noted a quote by **President Wilson,** which he made in his later years, pertaining to the Federal Reserve Act bill. **"I have unwittingly ruined my Country." President Wilson** dealing with the Federal Reserve Bank to help him get elected President cost the American people their freedom. In the year 1914, the **Federal Reserve Bank** (FRB) paid $20.60 for the paper that would be used by the **United States Bureau of Engraving and Printing (BEP)** to print one thousand Federal Reserve Notes. The denominations of the bills did not matter. The **Bureau of Engraving and Printing** would then give those printed Federal Reserve Notes to the **Federal Reserve Bank,** then they would route those notes to the government de facto to put into circulation. Those notes added up to several Trillions of dollars over the years. Please remember that for every **Federal Reserve Note** (FRN) that was put into circulation, the interest for using those **FRNs** had to be paid back to the **Federal Reserve Bank <u>in Gold</u>,** and <u>the terms of the contract could not be questioned</u>. How could **President Wilson** be so naive? The U.S. mint is still the only government agency that can coin gold, and other precious metals, which is real money.

2. The government de facto politicians sold out the American people a long time ago for the mighty <u>Federal Reserve Note</u> which the government de facto politicians could borrow anytime they wanted. The government de facto politicians never thought about the Gold Bars dwindling in Fort Knox until it was too late. Politicians only give a damn about voters when it is time for them to vote. In the author's opinion, when the **Federal Reserve Bank** owned most of Gold Bars in Fort Knox, the **Federal Reserve Bank** deliberately caused <u>the Great Stock Market Crash of 1929</u> that <u>led to the Great Depression, which led to the bankruptcy of the United States on March 9, 1933</u>. **One of the owners of the Federal Reserve Bank was the Lehman Brothers, who took advantage of the way the United States bankruptcy laws work. The Lehman Brothers filed for bankruptcy protection on September 15, 2008. This is the largest filing for bankruptcy protection in U.S. history. The Lehman Brothers had assets of over (Six Hundred Billion Dollars) $600,000,000,000 on record. How can any owner of the Federal Reserve Bank go bankrupt?** The author believes it may be impossible. Countries can only be Bankrupt for seventy (70) years. After seventy (70) years, the bankruptcy automatically discharges itself. That meant freedom for the government de facto. **<u>What about freedom for the American</u>**

**tax slaves**?

## THESE ARE SOME OF THE OWNERS OF THE FEDERAL RESERVE BANK

1. Chase Manhattan Bank of New York (Controlled by the Rockefellers)

2. Goldman Sachs Bank of New York

3. The Rothschild family is one of the most powerful, richest families in Europe, and on the Planet. The Rothschild family might be the biggest owner of the Federal Reserve Bank, which was 65% foreign-owned. For more in-depth information about the Federal Reserve Bank, read the book titled *VULTURE IN EAGLE'S CLOTHING*, or go on the internet to search for this information. Please remember that the government de facto and the Federal Reserve Bank could be responsible for corrupting the internet with fraudulent information. Please do not be deceived or fall for the **OKIE DOKE** anymore.

## PRESIDENT FRANKLIN D. ROOSEVELT DECLARES BANKRUPTCY OF THE UNITED STATE (See Congress James Traficant U.S. Bankruptcy Speech)

1. In 1929, the United State government de facto was almost depleted of gold bars, and that led to the Great Depression. The United States government de facto started bankruptcy proceedings way before the United States' bankruptcy was signed into law on March 9, 1933. The bankruptcy of the U.S. Government was officially declared by Congress and **President Franklin D. Roosevelt through Executive Orders 6072, 6012 and 6246.** (Also see H.J. Res. 1933 HR 1491 and 1933 HR 4960.) The United States government employees were ordered to turn in all of their **Gold Coins, Gold Bullion and Gold Certificates** to the Federal Reserve Banks, in exchange for Federal Reserve Notes. This was one of the requirements of the United States' Bankruptcy bail-out reorganization plan. The government de facto neglected to inform the American people that **President Roosevelt's Executive Order** was only for U.S. Citizens and was not mandated for any American Nationals of the 48 States, whom are governed by The Constitution of the United States of America.

## HOW PEOPLE BECAME COLLATERAL FOR THE GOVERNMENT DEBT

1. When we were fully created and discharged from our mothers' wombs, in a hospital, home, etc., people always made sure that a record of the baby's birth was recorded and maintained. This is now usually done by a Birth Certificate. The government de facto is now issuing your baby a Social Security Number with the Birth Certificate. These two government de facto documents are a direct links to the government de facto and its ownership of your baby. When your parents signed the birth certificate application, they unknowingly signed a self-adhesive contract that automatically sticks to them like self-adhesive tape. Your parents have unknowingly agreed to give their baby to the government de facto so the government de facto could now use the baby as collateral to borrow (Two Million, Five Hundred Thousand Dollars) $2,500,000 from the Federal Reserve Bank. The next thing that the government de facto might start doing to the babies is to secretly insert a **chip with a bar code number** into their bodies. If the parents were to find out about what the government de facto was doing, all the government de facto would have to tell the parents and the media is that the government has the right to protect babies from being kidnapped. The government de facto has your parents' signature on the contract (<u>the birth certificate application which is a contract</u>) that your parents signed freely, without using the UCC stamp on page 22. I know this may sound far-fetched, but so were the computer and the cell phone. A generation ago, many things were considered far-fetched. At one time, going to the moon was considered far-fetched. Please tell me why a government de facto agent can come into a home and take a child away from their parents? It's because the child is the property of the government de facto for 18 years, and the government de facto has the parents' signatures on its contract to prove that the child is the property of the government de facto. In 1933, when the United States government de facto filed for bankruptcy, the amount of Federal Reserve Notes that the government de facto could borrow from the Federal Reserve Bank, per birth certificate, was in the amount of (Five Hundred Thousand Dollars) $500,000. Every birth certificate on the planet is a negotiable instrument that, when registered with the government de facto, guarantees a specific amount of **FRNs** from the **Federal Reserve Bank**. The Constitution of the United States of America, **Article 1 Section 10** states, "No State shall... emit Bills of Credit." A bill of credit is a promissory note that most people have in their pocketbook or wallet, which is a promise to pay at a future time. The **Federal Reserve Bank** is not a government agency and **Article 1 Section 10** of the Constitution does not apply to corporations.

2. The author is telling the people the hard, cold, clear facts, but most people cannot deal with the truth. After the bankruptcy of 1933, the United States government de facto was financially broke and needed to negotiate the terms of borrowing more Federal Reserve Notes from the **Federal Reserve Bank**. The **FRB** had a plan for the American people, which was to make them into **tax slaves** for the United States' debt.

## PRESIDENT JOHN FITZGERALD KENNEDY IS THE GREATEST PRESIDENT OF THE 20TH CENTURY, WITHOUT A DOUBT

1. **President John Fitzgerald Kennedy** thought it was ludicrous for the Federal Government to pay a private corporation, the **Federal Reserve Bank**, interest in gold for using their private Federal Reserve Notes, which were printed by a government agency, the **Bureau of Engraving and Printing. President Kennedy** was not going to sell out his country, nor the American people, to the **British**. The **British** still control most of the wealth in many countries around the world. **For Example**: Who do you think has a Security Interest in the main goldmine in the **West African Country of Ghana**? Who do you think controls most of the **courts in America** that are run by Attorneys/Esquires? An Esquire is a rank that is immediately below Knight in **Britain**. Many **Presidents of the United States of America** were Esquires. **This is strictly forbidden by the true Thirteenth Amendment of the Constitution of the United States of America, also known as the TONA Amendment, which was fraudulently removed from many States' authentic copy of the Constitution of the United States of America.** The author loves **President Kennedy's** famous quote, "My Fellow Americans, ask not what your country can do for you. Ask what you can do for your country." The author of this **Powerful Manual** is trying to free the American people from bondage by telling them the truth, but most people cannot deal with the truth. "WAKE UP!"

2. In the year of 1963, **President Kennedy** signed Executive Order 11110, which ordered the <u>Secretary of the Treasury</u> to start reissuing Silver Certificates. This was the last time that Executive Order was enacted. The <u>Secretary of the Treasury</u> is the only government agency that can issue and control the flow of Silver Certificates, which were redeemed for silver up until the 1960s. Executive Order 11110 was never repealed by any President. **President Kennedy** challenged the two most successful vehicles on the planet that have been used to drive up the National Debt: war and the use of Private Federal Reserve Notes. **President Kennedy** was trying to squeeze the Federal Reserve Bank Notes out of existence. After **President Kennedy's** assassination, the **Private Federal Reserve Bank** squeezed the **Silver Certificates** out of

existence. My question to the reader is, "Why did the **Bureau of Engraving and Printing** stop printing Silver Certificates? Did the Secretary of the Treasury stop **BEP** from printing Silver Certificates?" **President Kennedy's** second plan was to have all of the American troops out of Vietnam by 1965. The majority of Congress, at the time of **President Kennedy's** assassination, were cowards and feared the **Federal Reserve Bank.** The **Bureau of Engraving and Printing** went back to printing Federal Reserve Notes just like that. How can the Secretary of the Treasury and Federal Reserve Bank, which was 65% foreign-owned, have enough power to override a President of the United States of America's Executive Order? The information in this **Powerful Manual** shall help all of the American people free themselves from bondage, thereby choosing the true and lawful **government de jure** that <u>**coexists**</u> with the **CORPORATE** government de facto.

## WESLEY SNIPES AND THE INTERNAL REVENUE SERVICE CODE

1. Movie actor, **Wesley Snipes,** went to prison for "willfully failing to file tax returns" with the Internal Revenue Service (IRS). As a government de jure American National, this is one of the most witless things that I have ever heard in my entire life. If **Snipes** is not mandated to file a tax return, he does not have to file a tax return. The reason why the 16th Amendment of the Constitution of the United States of America could not be lawfully ratified is because the increasing tax would come into direct conflict with <u>The Constitution of the United States of America Flat Tax</u>. The Flat Tax is a constitutional base tax, but when the Federal Reserve Act bill passed and was signed into law by **President Woodrow Wilson**, that created the first future **tax slaves** in America for the de facto government. (**See** "WHAT THE IRS DOES NOT WANT YOU TO KNOW ABOUT" **on page 76**.) If **Wesley Snipes** was a <u>government de jure American National</u>, he would have been protected by the <u>Constitution of the United States of America</u>. Please read this **Powerful Manual** carefully and never use an Attorney, unless you are a claimant/plaintiff in a lawsuit or need to appear before the magistrate if you got arrested. Then must follow the information page 36, 37, AND 38 titled <u>**IF YOU GET ARRESTED UNLAWFULLY**</u>.

## IF WESLEY SNIPES HAD KNOWN [THE REAL KING CHARLES]

1. If **Wesley Snipes** had known the author of this **Powerful Manual**, he never would have been incarcerated. First of all, the author would have advised him not to use an Attorney. All Attorneys are officers of the **government de facto**

**court**. That is the main reason that **Snipes** became liable to the IRS codes.

If **Snipes** had known the truth about the two governments and was a government de jure American National, he would have made a demand for proof of jurisdiction over person to be proven to exist as a fact of the law. As a government de jure American National, he would have won his case - hands down. If the government de facto court fails to prove jurisdiction over person as a fact of law, the <u>law states</u> **that the case must be dismissed for lack of jurisdiction**. In the IRS Code Book, income is considered profit, but people make equal pay for equal work and there is no profit to be made as it pertains to the people's labor. In a flat tax system there is no need for a Form W-4, which is really a self-adhesive contract that is very harsh on the people who violate the contract.

## THE REASON WHY WESLEY SNIPES WENT TO PRISON

1. The real reason that **Wesley Snipes** went to prison is because he used Attorneys <u>to represent him in a government de facto courtroom</u>. When anyone uses an Attorney to represent herself or himself in the courtroom, she or he agrees that they are a government de facto citizen. If they try to represent themselves in a government de facto courtroom, they shall also become liable to the government de facto court system for taking on the duties of an officer of the government de facto court. Any of these two options would have rendered **Snipes** liable to the government de facto court system. Many people believe that it is impossible for anyone to win against the Internal Revenue Service in a government de facto courtroom. **The author knows that all of those people are 100% wrong, because it is really quite simple to win if you are a government de jure American National.** The government de facto court cannot deny the people's Constitutional Rights. Furthermore, herein America, if a court fails to prove Jurisdiction over person as a fact of the law, the law states that the case must be dismissed for lack of jurisdiction over person. Do not ever represent yourself or use an Attorney to represent you. **The only time that you should use an Attorney, is to "<u>help you</u>" <u>appear before the magistrate</u> if you get arrested.** This is the only time that you should use an Attorney "to help you." <u>I did not say to defend you or to represent you</u> - **I want to make that very clear. Then, you must follow the information on pages 36, 37, and 38, titled <u>IF YOU GET ARRESTED UNLAWFULLY</u>.** The following phrases are the most powerful two phrases to use in any courtroom after you enact your Constitutional Rights. **"I am here under duress," and "I am making a demand for proof of Jurisdiction over person to be proven to exist as a fact of the law."**

2. The author believes that **Snipes'** Attorney might have sold him out, and the author is going to let the truth speak for itself. **Snipes** did not violate <u>The Constitution of the United States of America</u>. He violated a fraudulent, alleged Internal Revenue Service Code, which the author believes the IRS just added to the <u>IRS Code Book</u>. The IRS trickery made **Snipes** use an Attorney. Everyone knew that **Snipes** was very vocal about not paying taxes. If **Snipes** was a government de jure American National, he never would have served a day in prison. However, **Snipes** listened to and was persuaded by inexperienced wannabes. When you hear about celebrities or wealthy people having problem with the IRS, it usually relates to tax evasion, not for "willfully failing to file Tax Returns." That IRS Code even sounds ridiculous and if that is a new code that the IRS just added to its <u>Tax Code Book</u>, **Snipes'** Attorneys should have used the Grandfather Clause. **See** [BLACK'S LAW DICTIONARY: SIXTH EDITION (p. 699, ST. PAUL, MINN. WEST PUBLISHING CO. 1990). The Grandfather Clause is a "Provision in a new law or regulation exempting those already in or a part of the existing system which is being regulated."] If a new code or law came into effect that would stop a person from doing what they have been doing for years, the new code or law would not apply to them unless they adapted the new code or law into their life. **<u>The Constitution of the United States of America</u>** prohibits Congress from passing **ex-post facto laws - laws that make an act that was once legal, illegal.** This is herein accordance with Article 1, Section 10 of the Constitution. **Congress did not pass that fraudulent new IRS Code, the IRS did.** <u>The first obligation of all Attorneys is to the court</u>, <u>then the public</u>, <u>and then the client</u>. Check it out for yourself in **BLACK'S LAW DICTIONARY**. It's called <u>corpus juris secundum</u>. I would never trust or let any Attorney/Esquire defend me in any courtroom. All Attorneys are Esquires that have a duty to **Britain,** who licensed them to practice law. **<u>THE AUTHOR SHALL ELABORATE MORE ABOUT THAT STATEMENT ON PAGE 26 IN THIS MANUAL</u>.**

## THE INTERNAL REVENUE SERVICE IS NOT THAT POWERFUL

1. People often think and say that there is no way that anyone can win against the Internal Revenue Service. **<u>However, they are wrong</u>.** If you remember the author's statement on page 13, of this **Powerful Manual which is designed to show the reader "<u>the correct way to enter into any courtroom and never lose your Rights, Money, Freedom, Property or Life</u>."** This **Manual** will help the readers walk into any courtroom and never lose again in a government de facto court, which is really quite simple to do. One year, the author made over

(One Hundred Thousand Dollars) $100,000 [FROM] his labor and paid a very small amount of taxes. The last time the author filed a Tax Return is over twenty years [20] ago. The IRS would never take the author into any Federal courtroom, because the author is a government de jure American National with full, unimpaired rights and standing in the law. The IRS would get rocked - big time.

2. The Internal Revenue Service **Form W-4** is nothing more than a **self-adhesive contract** between the IRS, the government de facto, and the people who unknowingly sign the self-adhesive contracts without using the **UCC Sample Code below**. **The people must protect themselves against the trickery of the government de facto and the IRS.** Anyone who signs IRS **FORM W-4** without using the **Sample UCC Rubber Stamp** below will become liable to the IRS Codes. The government de facto and the IRS are the greatest manipulators of the truth and they do a great job of covering up the facts. The author is telling the American people - please do not fall for the government de facto and the IRS "OKIE DOKE" anymore and do not ever default on any document the IRS or the government de facto sends you because they will hold you accountable.

## SEE SAMPLE OF HOW TO FILL OUT FORM W-4 BELOW.

------------ Separate here and give Form W-4 to your employer. Keep the top part for your records. ------------

| Form **W-4**<br>Department of the Treasury<br>Internal Revenue Service | **Employee's Withholding Allowance Certificate**<br>► Whether you are entitled to claim a certain number of allowances or exemption from withholding is subject to review by the IRS. Your employer may be required to send a copy of this form to the IRS. | OMB No. 1545-0074<br>2017 |
|---|---|---|

1 Your first name and middle initial  *Charles*  Last name  *Jackson*     2 Your social security number  [ *123-55-7582* ]

Home address (number and street or rural route)  *2959 5th Avenue*

3 ☑ Single ☐ Married ☐ Married, but withhold at higher Single rate.
Note: If married, but legally separated, or spouse is a nonresident alien, check the "Single" box.

City or town, state, and ZIP code  *New York, New York [10029]*

4 If your last name differs from that shown on your social security card, check here. You must call 1-800-772-1213 for a replacement card. ► ☐

5 Total number of allowances you are claiming (from line H above or from the applicable worksheet on page 2)   5 | *80*
6 Additional amount, if any, you want withheld from each paycheck   6 | $
7 I claim exemption from withholding for 2017, and I certify that I meet **both** of the following conditions for exemption.
 • Last year I had a right to a refund of all federal income tax withheld because I had no tax liability, and
 • This year I expect a refund of all federal income tax withheld because I expect to have no tax liability.
If you meet both conditions, write "Exempt" here . . . . . . . ► | 7

Under penalties of perjury, I declare that I have examined this certificate and, to the best of my knowledge and belief, it is true, correct, and complete.

Employee's signature  *Charles Jackson*  Without Prejudice UCC 1-207 Anderson Version 1981 / Without Prejudice UCC 1-103 Supplemental Principles of Law
(This form is not valid unless you sign it.) ►     Date ►  *July 7, 2017*

8 Employer's name and address (Employer: Complete lines 8 and 10 only if sending to the IRS.) | 9 Office code (optional) | 10 Employer identification number (EIN)

For Privacy Act and Paperwork Reduction Act Notice, see page 2.    Cat. No. 10220Q    Form **W-4** (2017)

3. When you fill out a bank account application, **please make sure** that you always use the following **Sample UCC Rubber Stamp** below, on top or alongside your signature to protect your account from liens and levies.

**Sample UCC Rubber Stamp** Without Prejudice UCC 1-207 Anderson Version 1981
Without Prejudice UCC 1-103 Supplemental Principles of Law

## GOVERNMENT JOBS THAT MAKE YOU LIABLE FOR PAYING TAXES

1. These are some of the public servants and workers who are liable for paying taxes: Magistrates; Politicians; Police Officers; City Hospital Workers; Military Personnel; City, State, and Federal Office Employees; Fire Department Personnel; Government Sanitation Workers; Correction Officers, Government Licensed School Teachers, and Officers of Private Corporations. When you sign any document presented to you by the government de facto or their agents, you may be signing a self-adhesive contract, which automatically sticks to you, unknowingly. You must use the following code - <u>Without Prejudice UCC 1-207 Anderson Version 1981</u>, for you not to be liable to the government de facto contract and the **IRS** tax code. You must resubmit your Form W-4 with your employer with the UCC stamp, on page 22 through the top of your signature if you decide to switch governments and become a government de jure American National. **Please remember that you must file a UCC1.**

2. The government de facto does not have jurisdiction or any power over any government de jure American National. However, if you work for any branch of the government de facto, it is considered a privilege. The job application, along with the Form W-4 that you sign, will make you liable to the government de facto's self-adhesive contract. Because of that fact, you are liable to the IRS' tax code. The following are some of the essential government de facto LICENSES that are contracts: MARRIAGE LICENSE, DRIVER'S LICENSE, GUN LICENSE, etc. A note to the wise - when you fill out your next passport application, you should always write N/A (which means Not Applicable) where you are instructed to write in your Social Security Number, i.e. _ _ _ **N/A** _ _ _ _. I always do this, with no problem. You can use your passport to identify yourself, and that will give you a little more power. Remember: you've got to be wise. <u>You are not a citizen of New York State. You are a government de jure American National</u> - who domiciles in the New York Republic, for the record.

3. This is the way that the government de facto rule of law operates. If you agree with the government de facto rules of law, that is your right. Everyone is free to contract with whomever they choose to contract with. <u>The Constitution of the United States of America</u> recognizes a fair, flat tax. I am sure most Americans would be happy to pay a fair, flat tax. The American people should not be forced into compliance with the fraudulent IRS tax codes, especially when there was a time where over half of the money collected by the IRS was going into the banks of the most powerful families on the planet.

SEE NOTES FROM THE INTERNAL REVENUE SERVICE COMMISSIONERS FOR THE TAX YEARS OF 1992 AND 1993 BELOW. (The Key Words are: <u>Voluntarily</u> and <u>Voluntary Compliance</u> below).

---

The Internal Revenue Service Fraud

**Department of the Treasury**
**Internal Revenue Service**

## A NOTE FROM THE COMMISSIONER : 1992

Dear Tax Payer:

"As the Commissioner of the Internal Revenue, I want to thank you on behalf of the government of the United States and every American citizen...Thank you for paying your taxes. You are among the millions of Americans who comply with the tax law voluntarily."

*Shirley D. Peterson*

Shirley D. Peterson

**Department of the Treasury**
**Internal Revenue Service**

## A NOTE FROM THE COMMISSIONER : 1993

Dear Tax Payer:

"Thank you for making this nation's tax system the most effective system of voluntary compliance in the world...We have increased information and education efforts to help improve compliance, but we are also using traditional compliance efforts—examinations, collection and criminal enforcement—so that each person pays what he or she properly owes."

*Margaret Milner Richardson*

Margaret Milner Richardson

# HOW TO RESPOND TO ANY IRS OR DE FACTO GOVERNMENT NOTICE

a) First, stamp their documents with the "UCC Rubber Stamp."

b) Sign your name through the "UCC Rubber Stamp" with a red ink pen.

c) Then print the following quote (in #16 font) on their documents: I DO NOT CONSENT TO THIS NOTICE OR ACCEPT THIS CONTRACT OFFER BECAUSE OF FRAUD IN THE INCEPTION AND FRAUD FACTUM.

d) Then, print Fraudulent N/A in Red Ink (#22 font size).

Make three copies of the document for yourself and mail back the original document to the IRS, by Certified Mail. Make sure that you put the Certified Receipt Number on the first page of the document that you are sending back.

## If you do not respond, you will lose by default.

### MAKE YOUR UCC RUBBER STAMP (IN 6 OR 8 FONT SIZE)

Without Prejudice UCC 1-207 Anderson Version 1981
Without Prejudice UCC 1-103 Supplemental Principle of the Law

## IT IS ALL ABOUT COMMERCE (ELABORATION CONTINUED FROM PAGE 21

1. All courts must keep the money flowing into the court system. Before the American Revolutionary War was over with the British, there were concessions made and the British dictated the terms of the Treaty to end the war. <u>All commerce was to be handled by Esquires</u>. Every Attorney that passes the BAR is an Esquire. An Esquire is a British title that ranks right below Knight. All Attorneys/Esquires are British Subjects. The British and the Americans signed a Treaty to end the War, before the ratification of The Constitution of the United States of America. The Constitution states that all contracts made prior to the ratification of the United States Constitution remain valid. Article VI Clause 2, "This Constitution, and the Laws of the United States which shall be made in Pursuance thereof; and all Treaties made, or which shall be made, under the Authority of the United States shall be supreme Law of the Land; and the Judges in every State shall be bound thereby." The American Indian Tribes can use Article VI Clause 2 to obtain justice in the government de facto courtrooms. **The Court, the IRS, the Federal Reserve Bank, the British and Attorneys/Esquires** are all on the same team. <u>**Wesley Snipes** is a prime example, like so many others before him. You have to be wise.</u>

## THIS IS YOUR OPPORTUNITY TO START MAKING YOUR LIFE BETTER

1. Simply by going to a store like STAPLES or OFFICE DEPOT and purchase a black ink rubber stamp (like the sample below, in # 6 or 8 font). Sometimes, you may have to put the stamp through your signature so you should sign with a blue ink pen when possible. A red ink pen also works very well in the courtroom.

Sample: Without Prejudice UCC 1-207 Anderson Version 1981 Without
        Without Prejudice UCC 1-103 Supplemental Principles of Law

2. It is required to file a UCC1 FINANCING STATEMENT and Security Agreement with the Secretary of State. The Secretary of State is controlled by the Federal Government. There is nothing better than having the Federal Government and the Uniform Commercial Code (UCC) Processing Unit backing you up. The UCC is the most powerful code on the planet that covers international law. It is a <u>Federal Offense</u> if the code is violated. The UCC will give the Creditor total control of <u>**your Debtor's Properties**</u>. In criminal court, the debtor's name is mainly spelled in all capital letters, for example (<u>**JOHN DOE**</u>). Some civil courts are now spelling the debtor's name like this (<u>**John Doe**</u>), which indicates they are looking at you as a <u>**THING: a CORPORATION**</u>. A natural **person's name is spelled like this:** <u>John Prince Doe</u>. If you only have two names then you must state for the record in the court that you are <u>**John doe**</u> the natural person in

this matter

# UNIFORM COMMERCIAL CODE
## PROCESSING OFFICE

### FEES APPLICABLE TO THE UNIFORM COMMERCIAL CODE BUREAU
### <u>UCC FILINGS (UCC1, UCC3 OR UCC5)</u>

UCC Filing in paper-based format (including fax)                    $50.00

UCC Filing in a medium other than                                  $25.00

on paper or in paper based format

### <u>SEARCHES</u>

The fee for searching for filing against

One (1) debtor is                                                  $25.00

The fee for searching for filings against one

(1) debtor and issuing search results under seal is               $50.00

### UCC EXPEDITED HANDLING SERVICE

The fee for Expedited Service *(in addition                        $75.00

to the stated filing, search or copy fee)

*Expedited service means completion of the request on the day in which the request is received by the

UCC unit; requests for expedited service must be received by the UCC Unit at least two (2) hours prior to close of business.

November 7, 2018

### I am paying for the following

**Uniform Commercial Code**                    This UCC processing fee is for paper-based format- $50.00

**Processing Unit**                            Make payable to: NYS Department of State
**One Commerce Plaza,**
**99 Washington, Avenue, Suite 600**
**Albany, NY 12231**

**Uniform Commercial Code: (518) 474-4763**

# CONTRACT LAW

1. With the help of this **Powerful Manual**, you will be able to walk into any courtroom and protect yourself and your property from the tyranny of the government de facto. <u>Just do not let them con you, intimidate you, or trick you into giving them jurisdiction over person.</u> <u>The Constitution of the United States of America</u> gives everyone the right to contract, or not to contract, with whomever they please. Remember that you are not mandated to contract with the government de facto court.

2. The United States Supreme Court has been consistent on its rulings. No one possesses <u>the right</u> to force anyone into any contract therewith anyone else, including with the government de facto municipal corporations, like the United States Inc., or its myriad de facto political subdivisions, such as the State of New York, rather than the <u>New York Republic</u>, and the County of New York, rather than <u>New York County</u>. There is no requirement for anyone to consent with any government de facto contract.

## A NOTE FROM THE AUTHOR

This **Powerful Manual** is written to give the masses the knowledge, wisdom and strength to stand up and protect themselves, and their property, from the tyranny of the unjust government de facto. The author loves America and his freedom.

## NOTICE OF APPEARANCE

1. If you have a court appearance in any court, you should write a <u>Notice of Appearance</u> to the court. "For the record," I shall be appearing in Civil Housing Court, located at 111 Centre Street, specially and not generally on behalf of the debtor, <u>(DEBTOR'S NAME IS IN ALL CAPS)</u> **JOHN JOE DOE**, until this matter is resolved. [**BLACK'S LAW DICTIONARY: SIXTH EDITION** (p. 951, ST. PAUL, MINN. WEST PUBLISHING CO. 1990) defines Magistrates as "an inferior judicial officer; may be designated to hear a wide variety of motion and other pretrial matters in both criminal and civil cases. **With the consent of the parties.**"] I am not a juristic person, and Magistrate (<u>NAME IN ALL CAPS</u>) does not have my consent to hear the fraudulent case against me. I am a natural person, and I am making a demand for proof of jurisdiction over person to be proven to exist as a fact of the law. I shall be appearing in Housing Court located at 111 Centre Street, New York, New York [10013] under duress, until this matter is resolved in the creditor **John Joe Doe** favor."

2. After you send the magistrate a NOTICE OF APPEARANCE by CERTIFIED MAIL, you must make sure you appear in court on the right day and time. Do not be late! I am strongly advising you to go into the courtroom early to check it out for any side traps. When the Court Officer says, "All rise for the honorable JUDGE," I usually stand up and walk out of the courtroom for three seconds. You should always go into the courtroom with one or two other people who can bear witness for you. **Magistrate RUBEN A. MARTINO** dismissed a case against the author, telling the author, "This case is dismissed. Get out of my courtroom." The Author exited the courtroom, but he should have asked for a copy of the Court Order. One year later, they fraudulently evicted the author without a hearing or trial, and violated the Due Process of Law: Amendment V.

of the <u>Constitution of the United States of America</u>. **Magistrate MARTINO**

committed criminal fraud. In addition, the records of the author's last two court appearances were deleted from all of **Magistrate MARTINO**'s courtroom records. **Magistrate MARTINO** violated his Oath of Office and the laws. His fraudulent acts prompted the author to write this **informative, Powerful Manual** to teach people how to walk into any courtroom and never lose. This **Powerful Manual** teaches people how to **protect themselves.**

3. All magistrates must have your consent to trial you, but people usually give the magistrates their consent by what they do or say in the courtroom, so be very careful. When you make a demand for proof of jurisdiction over person in the courtroom, and if the magistrate fails to prove jurisdiction over person, the law states that the case must be dismissed for lack of jurisdiction but it really depends on you. However, when the author goes into any courtroom, the magistrates see the author's confidence and his power, and they respect him. <u>If you do not enact your Constitutional Rights</u> and show the Magistrate that you know what you are doing, and that you are the only creditor in the courtroom, the magistrate may have you going back and forth to court for a year, hoping that you miss an appearance and default. However, they shall eventually dismiss the case against you. You've got to let them know that you are the only creditor in the courtroom. (The creditor has the real power in all courtrooms, and all American Nationals are creditors.) You may have to make certain statements or do some things without disrupting the court. For example: you could look the magistrate in their eyes and raise your arms and whisper to ask what's going on. <u>**See sample of two notices of Appearance on pages 30-34.**</u>

# NOTICE OF APPEARANCE

| | |
|---|---|
| **SECURED PARTY** | ) |
| **JOHN JACKSON** | ) |
| | )     **INDEX NO. 11-0994 (AAD)** |
| **CLAIMANT** | ) |
| _____ | ) |

For the record, Secured Party is hereinafter known as
John Ben Jackson, Creditor/and Redemptor in this matter.


MAGISTRATE: ANTHONY A. DAVIS

1.   This statement is for the record. For the Claimant is "John Jackson" sentient, free-willed, natural person as defined therein Black's Law Dictionary Second and Sixth Edition, acting with the <u>rights of life,</u> upheld by all valid and just laws. I am John Jackson the Creditor/Redemptor in this matter, and shall be appearing special[ly] and not general[ly] on October 18, 2018 at the NEW YORK COUNTY CRIMINAL COURT at 60 Centre Street, 9:00 AM, on the behalf of the debtor until this matter is resolved. Without prejudice, all rights are reserved pertaining to the Constitution of the United States America. John Jackson is not a juristic person, and does not agree with any contract that is not made therein "favorite of the law" for the claimant as defined therein Black's Law Dictionary Second Edition.

## SAVACOOL V. BOUGHTON (5 Wend. 170. Supreme Court, New York, July, 1880)

1.   Magistrate ANTHONY A. DAVIS never proved jurisdiction over person and no one can Dispute SAVACOOL V. BOUGHTON (5 Wend. 170. Supreme Court, New York, July,1880) "By the court, Marcy, J. what an officer is required to show to justify himself in the execution of process is not very clearly settled. There is considerable contrariety of authority on the subject.  Where it appears on the face of the process that the court or magistrate that issued it had no jurisdiction of the subject-matter of the suit, or of the person of the party against whom it is directed, it is void, not only as respects the court or magistrate and the party at whose instance it is sued out, but it affords no protection to the officer who has acted under it." (1 of 3)

Marcy, J. goes on thereto state: "More strictness has been required in justifying under process of court of limited jurisdiction. Many cases may be found wherein it is stated generally that when an inferior court exceeds its jurisdiction, its proceedings are entirely void, and afford no protection to the court, the person or the officer who has executed its Process." The magistrate and the party at whose instance it is sued out, but it affords no protection to the office who has acted under it.

2. Marcy, J. goes on thereto state: "More strictness has been required in justifying under process of court of limited jurisdiction. Many cases may be found wherein it is stated generally that when an inferior court exceeds its jurisdiction, its proceedings are entirely void, and afford no protection to the court, the person or the officer who has executed its Process."

## DEMAND FOR PROOF OF JURICDICTION

1. It is a well-established principle of law that, once challenged, the person; the agency - whether federal, state, local, municipal or any department or instrumentality thereof asserting any form of jurisdiction must prove that jurisdiction to exist as a matter of law: Title 5, U.S. Code §-556 (d) states, as follows: When jurisdiction is challenged the burden of proof is on the government.

2. "Jurisdiction is essential to give validity to the determinations of administrative agencies, and where jurisdictional requirements are not satisfied, the action of the agency is a nullity..." City Street Improv. Co. v. Pearson 181 C 640, 185 P. 962. O'Neill v. Dept. of Professional & Vocational Standards 7 CA2d 393, 46 P2d 234. "No sanction can be imposed absent proof of jurisdiction." Standard V. Olesen, 74 S. Ct. 768. The following cases also substantiate the fact of law that the agency or person asserting jurisdiction must, when challenged, Prove that jurisdiction exists: McNutt v. G.M., Ct. 789, 80 L. Ed. 1135 Griffin v. Matthews, 310 Supp, 341, 423, F. 2d 272; Basso v. U.P.L., 495 F. 2d 906; 111 Thomson v. Gaskiel, 62 S. Ct. 673, 83L. Ed.

3. Our Supreme Court has ruled that "Because a court does not acquire jurisdiction by a mere recital contrary to what is shown in the record", the record of the case is the (Page 2 of 3) determining factor as to whether a court has jurisdiction. State Bank of Lake Zurich v. Thill, 113l.2d 294, 497 N.E.2d 1156 (1986).

4. Without the specific findings of jurisdiction by the court in an order or judgment, the order or judgment does not comply with the law and is void.

## NO STATUTE OF LIMITATIONS TO CHALLENGE A VOID ORDER

3.  Since a void order has no legal force or effect there can be no time limit within which to challenge the order or judgment. Further since the order has no legal force or effect, it can be repeatedly challenged, since no judge has the lawful authority to make a void order valid. Bates v. Board of Education, Allendale Community Consolidated School District No. 17, 136 Ill.2d 260, 267 (1990) (a court cannot confer jurisdiction where none existed and cannot make a void proceeding valid.); People ex rel. Gowdy v. Baltimore & Ohio R.R. Co., 385 Ill. 86, 92, 52 N.E.2d 255 (1943).

*CERTIFIED MAIL 6799 4432 0000 5599 8888*

*Secured Party*
John Ben Jackson

P.O. Box

421 8TH AVENUE

New York, New York [10031]

September 6, 2017

**SUBSCRIBED AND SWORN**

**(New York State)**

**BEFORE ME THIS_____DAY**          **ss**

_____ 2017          **(New York County)**    Without Prejudice UCC 1-207 Anderson Version 1981

_____          John Ben Jackson _____

Notary Signature          *(3 of 3)*

## NOTICE OF APPEARANCE

| | | |
|---|---|---|
| | ) | |
| **SECURED PARTY** | ) | **ROOM 334** |
| **BEN LEE** | ) | |
| | ) | **INDEX NO. 6067/2017 (MD)** |
| **CLAIMANT** | ) | |
| _____ | ) | |

For the record, SECURED PARTY is hereinafter known as
Ben Lee and Damaged Creditor in this matter.

MAGISTRATE: MICHELLE DAVIS

1. This statement is for the record. Without prejudice all rights are reserved pertaining to the Constitution of the United States of America. For the Claimant is "Ben Lee" sentient, free-willed, **natural person** as defined therein Black's Law Dictionary Second Edition, acting with the rights of life, upheld by all valid and just laws. Ben Lee is the creditor in this matter, and shall be appearing special[ly] and not general[ly] on the behalf of the debtor, thereon May 29, 2017 until this matter is resolved. The Secured Party is not a juristic person, and does not approve of any contract that pertains thereto the De facto Court located at 111 Centre Street.

2. BLACK'S LAW DICTIONARY, Sixth Edition, defined Magistrates as those who "May be designated to hear a wide variety of motions and other pretrial matters, in both criminal and civil cases, with the consent of the parties." I am not a juristic person, and Magistrate MICHELLE DAVIS does not have my consent thereto trial or to hear Case No. 6067/2017. I am making a demand for proof of jurisdiction over person and over subject matter to be proven to exist as a fact of the law.( Page 1 of 2)

3. No one can dispute SAVACOOL V. BOUGHTON (5 Wend. 170. Supreme Court, New York, July, 1880) Marcy, J. states, "What an officer is required to show to justify himself in the execution of process is not very clearly settled. There is considerable contrariety of authority on the subject. Where it appears on the face of the process that the court or magistrate that issued it had no jurisdiction of the subject-matter of the suit, or of the person of the party against whom it is directed, it is void, not only as respects the court or magistrate and the party at whose instance it is sued out, but it affords no protection to the officer who has acted under it."

4. Marcy, J. goes on thereto state: "More strictness has been required in justifying under process of court of limited jurisdiction. Many cases may be found wherein it is stated generally that when an inferior court exceeds its jurisdiction, its proceedings are entirely void, and afford no protection to the court, the person, or the officer, who has executed its Process."

*CERTIFIED MAIL 6799 4432 0000 5599 9876*

John Jackson

P.O. Box 338

Triborough Station

New York, New York [10035]

September 6, 2017

**SUBSCRIBED AND SWORN**

**(New York State)**

**BEFORE ME THIS_____DAY**          **(New York County)**

**(New York County)**

_____ 2017          **Without Prejudice UCC 1-207 Anderson Version 1981**

_____          Ben Lee _____

Notary Signature          (Page 2 of 2 )

## THINGS THAT YOU SHOULD KNOW BEFORE APPEARING IN COURT

1. On the first day of a Civil Court appearance, the court are now using a court clerk behind the **(bar)** to try to trap you into giving the court jurisdiction over person. So when you sign in, you must stop before the **(bar)** and tell the court clerk that you are going beyond the **(bar)** under duress. No court proceeding can move forward without your demand for proof of jurisdiction being proven to exist as a fact of the law. When you are in the courtroom, the court officer is going to call the Defendant's name, for example **JOHN DOE.** You should stand up and walk to the front of the court **and stop right before the (bar)** then say, "I am (your name) a Natural Person, and I am going beyond the <u>bar under duress</u>." Sometimes the **(bar)** is three feet from the entrance doorway, so be careful. **<u>If you do not say that you are going beyond the bar under duress, you will be giving the mediator or magistrate jurisdiction over person and she or he can and will judge you</u>. They have the court clerk behind the bar where you must go to sign in, so now you must tell the court clerk that you are going beyond the bar under duress before you sign in.** The bar can also be a swinging gate that a person must walk through, after the court officer calls the debtor's name; two pole-like objects on both sides of the courtroom; a barrier that separates the people from the judiciary; or a <u>door to a hearing room or conference room.</u> Then you should say these words, "<u>I am entering this conference room or hearing room under duress, and I am sitting down at this conference table</u> **under duress**." If anyone asks you to state your name at any time, you should say, "I am stating my name under duress, <u>**John Doe**</u>, and I am a natural person." If anyone asks you for your address, you should say, "I don't have an address. I domicile in the New York Republic, on the land that is commonly known as Manhattan (or Bronx, Queens, etc.)

2. When you are in the courtroom and the Court Officer calls the debtor's name, you should stand up, **walk up to the front of the court and stop before bar and say, "<u>I am [your name] natural person and I am going beyond the bar under duress</u>.** The magistrate may try to trick you and say to the court officer**, "Where is the defendant?"** You should not respond because the magistrate is not talking to you or about you. The magistrate is talking about the debtor, "<u>JOHN DOE</u>." Then, you should say, "I am here on behalf of that person, I am the only creditor in this matter, and I am here <u>under duress</u>." The magistrate may say, "You know that's you," and then you should respond with, "My name is spelled Capital J, small o-h-n and Capital D, small o-e. I am a **<u>Natural Person</u>** as defined in **BLACK'S LAW DICTIONARY: SECOND EDITION** acting with the rights of life, upheld by all valid and just laws." The author believes that before you go into any courtroom you must practice these

techniques and be prepared for everything.

3. **Never call the magistrate a "Judge" or "Your Honor." If you do, you will be giving the magistrate jurisdiction over person and she or he can and will judge you.** Do not call them anything. However, if a magistrate or hearing examiner insists that you call her or him "Judge" or "Your Honor," then you should ask the magistrate, "to please tell me the name of the president of the United States of America that appointed you that honor of being Judge?" If she or he was not appointed by the President of the United States of America, then you should say to the magistrate, "You are just a magistrate and you just committed perjury on the bench." **President Abraham Lincoln** was the last de jure Constitutional elected President that appointed Article Three Judges, which are real Court Judges. The next request that you should ask of the magistrate is to see her or his Certificate of Oath of Office.

4. **This is very important:** If the magistrate or hearing examiner directs you to raise your right hand and says, "I am going to swear you in first," Your response should be, "In every court in America, a demand for proof of jurisdiction must be proven to exist first as a fact of the law, before any court proceedings can move forward". If the magistrate threatens to charge you with contempt of court (if you do not raise your right hand to be sworn in), then you should raise your right hand and after the person who is swearing you in has finished talking, you should say, "I am swearing in under duress." If a magistrate tells you to approach the bench, then you must say, "I am approaching the bench under duress."

5. If any officer of the court speaks out and says that you are pleading "innocent" or "guilty" you should say, "I am not pleading anything until my demand for proof of jurisdiction over person has been proven to exist as a fact of the law."

## IF YOU GET ARRESTED UNLAWFULLY

1. A Legal Aid Attorney is going to come to the holding cell and talk to you, so talk to her or him and say [that you did not do anything wrong and that the police officers fraudulently arrested you, for no reason, and that you did not violate any laws]. The author cannot really tell you what to say, however if you are seeking to be a government de jure American National like me, you have to be wise. I do not know what will happen to you in the future and this is only an EXAMPLE of what I might say to the Legal Aid Attorney. However, when you go into the courtroom, the District Attorney, is going to state the case against

you. So, do not ever talk to any District Attorney, because she or he is not there to help you. When you are in the courtroom, and as soon as the District Attorney finishes stating the case against you, you should say these words: "<u>For the record</u>: **All rights are reserved, pertaining to the Constitution of the United States of America; The Uniform Commercial Code UCC 1-207 Anderson Version 1981. I do not agree with any contract that is pertaining to this court, and I am here under duress.**" "**I am making a demand for proof of jurisdiction over person to be proven to exist as a fact of the law.**" **Note**: You may not be able to complete the above quotes, in full, at one time.

2. **The Magistrate might try to trick you, and say to you, "Do you <u>understand the charges against you</u>?" <u>If you say that you do, you just agreed to the charges, and you are now liable for those charges</u>.** You should say, "<u>No, I do not understand the charges against me, but I know what you are trying to do</u>." Then, the Magistrate might say to you, "So you do understand the charges against you?" Your response should be, "<u>I said that I do not understand the charges against me, for the record</u>. I am making a demand for proof of jurisdiction over person to be proven to exist as a fact of the law." Do not sign any documents, but if you must, always write above your signature, "Without Prejudice UCC 1-207 Anderson Version 1981" on every document that you sign, inside or outside the courtroom. Almost all government documents are contracts, which are known as "self-adhesive contracts." As I mentioned earlier court mainly spells the debtor's name in all Capital letters: for example **JOHN HENRY DOE**. The real way to spelling a natural person's name is like this: **<u>John Henry Doe</u>**. The court cannot spell out your first, middle and family name in upper, lower case letters. Names in all capital letters are corporate names; please look at the debtors' Driver's License, Birth Certificate, Social Security Card and other government IDs. The debtor owns everything and the courts can only deal with you as a Corporation because only Corporations can deal with Corporations. If you agree that you are a Corporation, you are a fictional person and a debtor. This is the government de facto Corporate America that we are all part of now, either directly or indirectly. In criminal court, if an Attorney shows you any paper from the court with your name spelled in upper and lower case letters, it is a fraudulent trick, so do not fall for the OKIE DOKE. Just follow the directions in this **Powerful Manual** and do not ever be swayed. If you are incarcerated for any length of time, you can file a tort claim against the city for one million dollars for constitutional rights violation. Just remember that your Constitutional rights must be enacted.

3. The law states that whoever is ascertaining jurisdiction, <u>when challenged</u>, must prove that jurisdiction exists over person and over subject matter as a fact of the law.  That means the court must obtain jurisdiction over subject matter and over person to gain jurisdiction over you to trial you; if either is lacking the case must be dismissed. When a court fails to prove jurisdiction over person, the court automatically loses jurisdiction over subject matter, and the case must be dismissed for lack of jurisdiction.

## MORE TRICK QUESTIONS THAT A CLERK OR MAGISTRATE MIGHT ASK YOU

1. "What is your address?" Your response to that question should be, for example, "I don't have an address: <u>I domicile at 2045, Fifth Avenue in the New York Republic on the land that is commonly referred to as Manhattan (the Bronx, Brooklyn</u>, etc)." All addresses are incorporated because of the state abbreviation **NY** and the Zip Code. "What is your telephone number?" You should say, "Without prejudice all rights are reserved pertaining to the Constitution of the United States of America," and "I am exercising my right not to answer that question."

2. All telephone numbers are incorporated, and you must spell out the City and the State, i.e. New York, New York. Do not ever use the abbreviation "NY." Always put **square brackets** around the Zip Code **[10032]** and your Telephone Number **[212 446-8878] when you write it on paper. Please try to make this new way of protecting yourself into a <u>habit</u>. Square brackets MEAN THAT YOU CAN SEE IT, BUT IT IS NOT REALLY THERE, PERTAINING TO THE LAW.**

3. "What is your income?" Your response should be, "I am exercising my right not to answer that question." If a magistrate ever says to you, "This is not a trial and you cannot take the Fifth Amendment," your response should be, "I did not say that I was taking the Fifth Amendment; I said that I am exercising my right not to answer that question."

## QUESTIONS YOU MAY OR MAY NOT WANT TO ASK A MAGISTRATE, AND YOUR REMARKS

1. "Are the Federal **Rules of Civil Procedure** binding in this Court?" The next request you should ask of the magistrate, "I would like to see your Certificate of Oath of Office." If the magistrate stands up and walks off the bench, without saying anything, you should wait one minute and then you should stand up and say, "I guess there is no court going on here today." Then exit the courtroom because your case is over.


2. If the magistrate is still on the bench, the next question that you should ask is, "What is the flag under which you are operating?" Wait for her or his response, although she or he may not answer that question. Then, you should point to the flag in the courtroom and say, "That flag is described in Army regulation 840-10 chapter 4-3, where they allow Yellow Fringe on a Military Flag. Since I was never in the Military, you cannot conduct a Military Tribunal against a de jure American National. Because you have surrendered by elevating a Yellow Fringed Flag or Tasseled Flag in the New York Republic, you are guilty of committing treason against the United States of America, against the Constitution of the United of America, and against the American Constitutional Flag. <u>The Constitutional Flag of the United States of America</u> is described in Title 4 USC 11.9. The next question you should ask the magistrate: "Is this an **IN REM COURT**," which means Bankruptcy Court. Ever since 1933, after President Franklin D. Roosevelt declared the Bankruptcy of the United States, all courts have been Bankruptcy Courts and may still be Bankruptcy Courts. I really don't believe that the United States government de facto re-filed bankruptcy of the United States. After **the 70 year Bankruptcy time limitation had expired, ending the United States' Bankruptcy**. The government de facto fought a war in Afghanistan and another war in Iraq. These two wars cost over two trillion dollars. I also believe that the British Powers are going to try to make President Donald J. Trump file Bankruptcy for the United States. My question is, how and when?

## IMPORTANT NOTICE ABOUT CIVIL HOUSING COURT

The author went to Civil Housing Court and the court clerk asked him how much rent he owed. The author relayed that he did not owe any money. The author went into the courtroom and made a demand for proof of jurisdiction over person to be proven to exist as a fact of the law. The author informed the magistrate that no court proceeding can move forward without it. The author already had a lien on his property in the amount of One Million ($1,000,000) Dollars with an Adverse Claim that is good for the next five years. *Now that is being secure.*

## LET'S GO BACK IN TIME TO 1933 TO DISCUSS THE BANKRUPTCY OF THE UNITED STATES AND THE REASON BEHIND 9/11/2001

1. In 1933, almost all of the States gave up their land as collateral to bail out the United States Government de facto. The one exception was the State of Texas. The State of Texas was oil-rich and refused to give up its land to bail out the United States Government de facto. That means all of the land in America, except for the State of Texas, was given to the Federal Reserve Bank as collateral to bail out the United States. Consequently, almost all of the land that the American people believe they own was really owned by the Federal Reserve Bank. That is the main reason why people pay land taxes/rent.

2. The United States government de facto can only be bankrupt for 70 years, and then the bankruptcy automatically discharges itself. Let me say that again - The United States government de facto can only be bankrupt for 70 years. I don't know when the bankruptcy negotiation began, but I do know when the bankruptcy negotiation ended - March 9, 1933. Now you might understand a little more about why September 11, 2001 happened, and the evil money powers behind that evil attack to keep the United States in debt. The war with Afghanistan ended too quickly, and that is why I believe the money powers of the World made President George Walker Bush invade Iraq.

## SEE COPY OF THE FOREBODING (TWENTY) $20 BILL ON THE NEXT PAGE

1. Do you really believe that the Twenty Dollar bill's picture of the burning World Trade Center and The Pentagon is a coincidence? If you really believe that, then I would like to sell you the Brooklyn Bridge! I am telling the American people to wake up, because they have been sleeping for too long. We should be free from the contract that was signed with the British to end the war for independence, that was signed before The Constitution of the United States of America was even ratified. Martin Luther King Jr. said, "No lie can last forever." The World Court is an option that can be used in filing a claim against the British Terrorists for Justice. The British breached the Contracts it had with the Americans to end the war for independence.

2.  The Money Powers of the world have their own simplistic way of recording their history, and it is right in our faces, but someone let the cat out of the bag. The American people are so brainwashed and gullible and always fall the "OKIE DOKE". The foreboding (twenty) $20 dollar bill is no coincidence. The attack on America was well orchestrated. The British breached the contract they had with Americans before the Constitution of the United States of America was ratified. <u>We the People</u> must be free from the British Terrorists

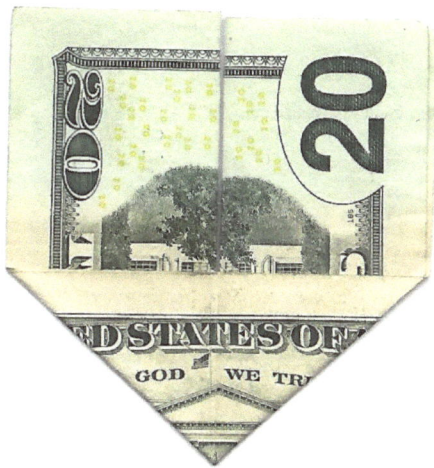

# THE NEXT PAGES ARE CASES RELEVANT TO JURISDICTION

## ACTING WITHOUT JURISDICTION

### *ORDERS, DECISIONS, ALL ACTS IN THE COURT ARE VOID EVEN BEFORE REVERSAL*

1.   The law is well settled that a void order or judgment is void even before reversal. Vallely **v.** Northern Fire & Marine Ins. Co., 254 U.S. 348, 41 S.Ct. 116 (1920) ("Courts are constituted by authority and they cannot go beyond that power delegated to them. If they act beyond that authority, and certainly in contravention of it, their judgments and orders are regarded as nullities. They are not voidable, but simply VOID, AND THIS EVEN PRIOR TO REVERSAL." [Emphasis added]); Old Wayne Mut. I. Assoc. v. McDonough, 204 U.S. 8, 27 S.Ct. 236 (1907); Williamson v. Berry, 8 How. 495, 540, 12 L.Ed. 1170, 1189 (1850); Rose v. Himely, 4 Cranch 241, 269, 2 L.Ed. 608, 617 (1808).

2. Should the judge not have subject-matter jurisdiction, then the law states that the judge has not only violated the law, but is also a trespasser of the law. Von Kettler et.al. v. Johnson, 57 Ill. 109 (1870) ("if the magistrate has not such jurisdiction, then he and those who advise and act with him, or execute his process, are trespassers.");Elliott v. Peirsol, 1 Pet. 328, 340, 26 U.S. 328, 340 (1828) ("Without authority, its judgments and orders are regarded as nullities. They are not voidable, but simply void; and form no bar to a recovery sought, even prior to a reversal in opposition to them. They constitute no justification; and all persons concerned in executing such judgments or sentences, are considered, in law, as trespassers. This distinction runs through all the cases on the subject; and it proves, that the jurisdiction of any court exercising authority over a subject, may be inquired into in every court, when the proceedings of the former are relied on and brought before the latter, by the party claiming the benefit of such proceedings."); In re TIP-PA-HANS Enterprises, Inc., 27 B.R. 780, 783 (1983) (a judge "lacks jurisdiction in a particular case until it has been demonstrated that jurisdiction over the subject matter exists") (when a judge acts "outside the limits of his jurisdiction, he becomes a trespasser ...") ("... courts have held that where courts of special or limited jurisdiction exceed their rightful powers, the whole proceeding is coram non-judice ...").

3. Trespasser is defined in Black's Law Dictionary (6th Edition) as one who has committed  unlawful interference with one's person, property, or rights.

4. If a judge acts without subject-matter jurisdiction, the judge is acting unlawfully, he/she has committed an unlawful interference with one's person, property, or rights.

5. A judge who acts without subject-matter jurisdiction in anything but common criminal? All orders and judgments issued by a judge, who acts  without subject-matter jurisdiction are void, as a matter of the law.

6. As the supreme Court summed it up: "If any Tribunal (Court) finds absence of proof of Jurisdiction over the person and subject matter, the case must  be dismissed". Louisville RR v. Motley, 211 US 149, 29 S. Ct. 42

Lack Jurisdiction

## ELEMENTS OF LACK OF JURISDICTION

7. In courts of limited jurisdiction, subject-matter jurisdiction is determined only by an inspection of the record of the case. The inspection of the record of the case must show that all of the elements of subject-matter jurisdiction existed, and existed at all times. State Bank of Lake Zurich v. Thill, 113 Ill.2d 294, 497 N.E.2d 1156 (1986); Herb v. Pitcairn, 384 Ill. 237, 241 (1943); People ex rel. Curtin v. Heizer, 36 Ill.2d 438, 223 N.E.2d 128 (1967); Brown v. VanKeuren, 340 Ill. 118, 122 (1930); Wabash Area Development, Inc. v. Ind. Com., 88 Ill.2d 392 (1981). Either subject-matter jurisdiction exists, or it doesn't.

8. If subject-matter jurisdiction is denied, it must be proved by the party claiming that the court has subject matter jurisdiction as to all of the requisite elements of subject-matter jurisdiction. A partial list of the elements in which the Court is without subject-matter jurisdiction and all of its orders/judgments are void:

(1) No Petition in the record of the case, Brown v. VanKeuren, 340 Ill. 118, 122 (1930),

(2) Defective Petition filed, Brown v. VanKeuren, 340 Ill. 118, 122 (1930),

(3) Fraud committed in the procurement of jurisdiction, Fredman Brothers Furniture v. Dept. of Revenue, 109 Ill.2d 202, 486 N.E.2d 893 (1985),

(4) Fraud upon the court, In re Village of Willowbrook, 37 Ill.App.3d 393 (1962),

(5) A judge does not follow statutory procedure, Armstrong v. Obucino, 300 Ill. 140, 143 (1921),

(6) Unlawful activity of a judge, Code of Judicial Conduct,

(7) Violation of due process, Johnson v. Zerbst, 304 U.S. 458, 58 S.Ct. 1019 Pure Oil Co. v. City of Northlake, 10 Ill.2d 241, 245, 140 N.E.2d 289 (1956); Hallberg v. Goldblatt Bros., 363 Ill. 25 (1936),

(8) If the court exceeded its statutory authority, Rosenstiel v. Rosenstiel, 278 F.Supp. 794 (S.D.N.Y. 1967),

(9) Any acts in violation of 11 U.S.C. §362(a),In re Garcia, 109 B.R. 335 (N.D. Illinois, 1989),

(10) Where no justifiable issue is presented to the court through proper pleadings, Ligon v. Williams, 264 Ill.App.3d 701, 637 N.E.2d 633 (1st Dist. 1994),

(11) Where a complaint states no cognizable cause of action against that party, Charles v. Gore, 248 Ill.App.3d 441, 618 N.E.2d 554 (1st Dist. 1993),

(12) Where any litigant was represented before a court by a person/law firm that is prohibited by law to practice law in that jurisdiction,

(13) When the judge is involved in a scheme of bribery (the Alemann cases, Bracey v. Warden, U.S. Supreme Court No. 96-6133 (June 9, 1997),

Lack of Jurisdiction

(14) Where a summons was not properly issued,

(15) Where service of process was not made pursuant to statute and Supreme Court Rules, Janove v. Bacon, 6 Ill.2d 245, 249, 128 N.E.2d 706, 708 (1955),

(16) When the Rules of the Circuit Court of Cook County are not complied with,

(17) When the Local Rules of the Domestic Relations Division, Cook County, Illinois are not complied with,

(18) Where the judge does not act impartially, Bracey v. Warden, U.S. Supreme Court No. 96-6133 (June 9, 197),

(19) Where the statute is vague, People v. Williams, 638 N.E.2d 207 (1st Dist. 1994),

(20) When proper notice is not given to all parties by the movant, Wilson v. Moore, 13 Ill.App.3d 632, 301 N.E.2d 39 (1st Dist. 1973),

(21) Where an order/judgment is based on a void order/judgment, Austin v. Smith, 312 F.2d 337, 343 (1962); English v. English, 72 Ill.App.3d 736, 393 N.E.2d 18 (1st Dist. 1979), or

(22) Where the public policy of the State of Illinois is violated, Martin-Tregona v. Roderick, 29 Ill.App.3d 553, 331 N.E.2d 100 (1st Dist. 1975).

All of the above elements must be met before the court is conferred with subject-matter jurisdiction. Should any element not be complied with, the judge is without subject-matter jurisdiction; his/her orders and judgments are void, of no legal force or effect.

Lack of Jurisdiction

## SUBJECT MATTER JURISDICTION-JURISDICTION IN PERSONAM

1. Judicial jurisdiction is the authority of a court to hear and decide an action and authority Black's Law Dictionary, 5th Ed. Cites the following legal definition for Jurisdiction in personam; Power which a court has over the defendant's person and which is required before a court can enter a personal or in personam judgment. Pennoyer v. Neff, 95 U.S. 714, 24 L. Ed. 565. It may be acquired by an act of the defendant within a jurisdiction under a law by which the defendant impliedly consents to the personal jurisdiction of the court. Hess v. Pawloski, 274 U.S. 352, 47 S. Ct. 632, 71 L. Ed. 1091.

2. The Supreme Court ruled in 1970: "Waivers of Constitutional Rights not only must be Voluntary, they must be Knowingly Intelligent Acts done with Sufficient Awareness of the Relevant Circumstances and Consequences." Brady v. U.S. 742 at 747   37. The affiant does not waive any state or federal constitutional rights.

3. Jurisdiction in personam or over person may be acquired by an act of the defendant within a jurisdiction under a law by which the defendant impliedly consents to the personal jurisdiction of the court.   Hess v. Pawloski, 274 U.S. 352, 47 S. Ct. 632, 71 L. Ed. 1091 Black's Law Dictionary, 5th Ed.

4. Judicial jurisdiction is the authority of a court to hear and decide an action and authority to prosecute. Legislative jurisdiction is: the authority of and legislative body to pass legislation that is binding. Before a court can act or a legislature enforces compliance, each agency must have jurisdiction over both person and the subject matter. If either is wanting, the court or legislature is without jurisdiction the case must be dismissed or the legislation then becomes null and void. This is a matter of law.

5. Courts are without authority to adjudicate a matter over which it has no jurisdiction even though a court may possess jurisdiction over the parties to the litigation. "No sanction can be imposed absent proof of jurisdiction."
- Stanard v. Olesen, 74 S. Ct. 768

6. Once Challenged, Jurisdiction Cannot Be "Assumed", It Must Be Proved To Exist! Stuck v. Medical Examiners, 94 Ca2d 751. 211 P2s 389. "Jurisdiction once challenged cannot be assumed and must be decided." Maine v. Thiboutot 100 S. Ct 2502, "... jurisdiction cannot be assumed, but must be clearly shown." Brooks v. Yawkey 200 F. 2d. 633

7. It is a well-established principle of law that, once challenged, the person, agency whether federal, state, local, municipal or any department or instrumentality thereof asserting any form of jurisdiction must prove that jurisdiction to exist as a matter of law: Title 5, U.S. Code §-556 (d) states, as follows: When jurisdiction is challenged the burden of proof is on the government.

8. "Jurisdiction is essential to give validity to the determinations of administrative agencies and where jurisdictional requirements are not satisfied, the action of the agency is a nullity..." City Street Improv. Co. v. Pearson 181 C 640, 185 P. 962. O'Neill v. Dept. of Professional & Vocational Standards 7 CA2d 393, 46 P2d 234. "No sanction can be imposed absent proof of jurisdiction." Standard V. Olesen, 74 S. Ct. 768. The following cases also substantiate the fact of law that the agency or person asserting jurisdiction must, when challenged, Prove that jurisdiction exists: McNutt v. G.M., Ct. 789, 80 L. Ed. 1135Griffin v. Matthews, 310 Supp, 341, 423, F. 2d 272; Basso v. U.P.L. 495 2d 906; 111 Thomson v. Gaskiel, 62 S. Ct. 673, 83L. Ed.

9. Proof of Jurisdiction must appear on the record as a fact of law. "The Law requires Proof of Jurisdiction to appear on the record of the administrative agency and all administrative proceedings". Hagans v. Lavine, 415 U.S. 533 "Therefore, it is necessary that the record present the fact establishing the jurisdiction of the tribunal". Lowe v. Alexander 15C 296; People v. Board of delegates of S. F. Fire Dept. 14 C 479.

Acting Without Jurisdiction

## NO PRESUMPTION OF JURISDICTION

1. While in a court of general jurisdiction, there is a presumption that the judge has subject-matter jurisdiction, such is not the case in courts of limited jurisdiction. In all courts of limited jurisdiction, there is no presumption of subject-matter jurisdiction.

2. In all courts of limited jurisdiction, the record of the case must support any
claim of subject-matter jurisdiction. If subject-matter jurisdiction does not appear from the record of the case, the presiding judge is acting without subject-matter jurisdiction and his/her orders are void, of no legal force or effect. State Bank of Lake Zurich v. Thill, 113 Ill.2d 294, 497 N.E.2d 1156 (1986)

3. Wabash Area Development, Inc. v. Ind. Com., 88 Ill.2d 392 (1981) ("that compliance with the statutory requirements for the issuance of the writ must affirmatively appear in the record."); I.C.R.R. Co. v. Hasenwinkle, 232 Ill. 224, 227 (1908) ("The law presumes nothing in favor of the jurisdiction of a court exercising special statutory powers, such as those given by statute under which the court acted, (Chicago and Northwestern Railway Co. v. Galt, 133 Ill. 657), and the record must affirmatively show the facts necessary to give jurisdiction. The record must show that the statute was complied with"); In re Marriage of Stefiniw, 253 Ill.App.3d 196, 625 N.E.2d 358 (1st Dist. 1993) ("A judgment is characterized as void and may be collaterally attacked at any time where the record itself furnished the facts which establish that the court acted without jurisdiction."); People v. Byrnes, 34 Ill.App.3d 983, 341 N.E.2d 729 (2nd Dist. 1975)

4. ("Whereas a court of general jurisdiction is presumed to have jurisdiction to render any judgment in a case arising under the common law, there is no such presumption of jurisdiction in cases arising under a specific statutory grant of authority. In the later cases the record must reveal the facts which authorize the court to act."); Zook v. Spannaus, 34 Ill.2d 612, 217 N.E.2d 789 (1966) ("In the absence of such findings in the record and in the absence of any evidence in the record to support such findings the court was without jurisdiction in this special statutory proceeding to enter an order authorizing the guardian to consent to adoption.");Fico v. Industrial Com., 353 Ill. 74 (1933) ("Where the court is exercising a special statutory jurisdiction the record must show upon its face that the case is one where the court has authority to act.").

5. The judge has a duty to continually inspect the record of the case, and if subject-matter jurisdiction does not appear at any time from the record of the case, then he has the duty to dismiss the case as lacking subject-matter
jurisdiction. Should a judge act in any case in which he does not have subject-matter jurisdiction, he is acting unlawfully, U.S. v. Will, 449 U.S. 200, 216, 101 S.Ct. 471, 66 L.Ed.2d 392, 406 (1980); Cohens v. Virginia, 19 U.S. (6 Wheat) 264, 404, 5 L.Ed 257 (1821), and without any judicial authority.

## WHEN A PARTY DENIES JURISDICTION

1. In a court of limited jurisdiction, whenever a party denies that the court has subject matter jurisdiction, it becomes the duty and the burden of the party claiming that the court has subject-matter jurisdiction to provide evidence from the record of the case that the court holds subject-matter jurisdiction. Bindell v. City of Harvey, 212 Ill.App.3d 1042, 571 N.E.2d 1017 (1st Dist. 1991) ("the burden of proving jurisdiction rests upon the party asserting it."); Loos v. American Energy Savers, Inc., 168 Ill.App.3d 558, 522 N.E.2d 841 (1988) ("Where jurisdiction is contested, the burden of establishing it rests upon the plaintiff.").

2. Until the plaintiff/petitioner submits uncontroverted evidence of subject matter jurisdiction to the court that the court has subject-matter jurisdiction, the court is proceeding without subject-matter jurisdiction. Should the plaintiff/petitioner not provide uncontroverted evidence of subject-matter jurisdiction, all orders or judgments issued by the judge are void ab initio. A judge should not proceed in any action in which the judge does not have subject
-matter jurisdiction, since he/she has no lawful authority to act.

Acting Without Jurisdiction

3. The law places the duty and the burden upon the plaintiff/petitioner. Should the court attempt to place the burden upon the defendant/respondent, the court has acted against the law, violates the defendant/respondent's due process rights, and the judge under court decisions has immediately lost subject-matter jurisdiction.

## COURT MUST PROCEED ACCORDING TO LAW OR STATUTE

1. In a court of limited jurisdiction, the court must proceed exactly according to the law or statute under which it operates. Flake v. Pretzel, 381 Ill. 498, 46 N.E.2d 375 (1943) ("the actions, being statutory proceedings, ... were void for want of power to make them.") ("The judgments were based on orders which were void because the court exceeded its jurisdiction in entering them. Where a court, after acquiring jurisdiction of a subject matter, as here, transcends the limits of the jurisdiction conferred, its judgment is void."); Armstrong v. Obucino, 300 Ill. 140, 143, 133 N.E. 58 (1921) ("The doctrine that where a court has once acquired jurisdiction it has a right to decide every question which arises in the cause, and its judgment or decree, however erroneous, cannot be collaterally assailed, is only correct when the court proceeds according to the established modes governing the class to which the case belongs and does not transcend in the extent and character of its judgment or decree the law or statute
which is applicable to it."

2. Whenever a judge does not exactly comply with the statute, he/she has lost subject-matter jurisdiction and all orders or judgments issued without subject-matter jurisdiction are void, of no legal force or effect.

## IN COURTS OF LIMITED JURISDICTION,

## ALL ORDERS MUST CONTAIN THE SPECIFIC

## FINDINGS THAT THE COURT HAS JURISDICTION

1. All orders or judgments issued by a judge in a court of limited jurisdiction must contain the findings of the court showing that the court has subject-matter jurisdiction, not allegations that the court has jurisdiction. In re Jennings, 68 Ill.2d 125, 368 N.E.2d 864 (1977) ("in a special statutory proceeding an order must contain the jurisdictional findings prescribed by statute."); Zook v. Spannaus, 34 Ill.2d 612, 217 N.E.2d 789 (1966).

2. Our Supreme Court has ruled that "Because a court does not acquire jurisdiction by a mere recital contrary to what is shown in the record", the record of the case is the determining factor as to whether a court has jurisdiction. State Bank of Lake Zurich v. Thill, 113 Ill.2d 294, 497 N.E.2d 1156 (1986).

3. A judge's allegation that he has subject-matter jurisdiction is only an
allegation (Lombard v. Elmore, 134 Ill.App.3d 898, 480 N.E.2d 1329 (1st Dist. 1985); Hill v. Daily, 28 Ill.App.3d 202, 204, 328 N.E.2d 142 (1975)); inspection of the record of the case has been ruled to be the controlling factor. If the record of the case does not support subject-matter jurisdiction, then the judge has acted without subject-matter jurisdiction. The People v. Brewer, 328 Ill. 472, 483 (1928) "If it could not legally hear the matter upon the jurisdictional paper presented, its finding that it had the power can add nothing to its authority, – it had no authority to make that finding".

4. Without the specific findings of jurisdiction by the court in an order or judgment, the order or judgment does not comply with the law and is void.

Acting Without Jurisdiction

## NO STATUTE OF LIMITATIONS TO CHALLENGE A VOID ORDER

1. Since a void order has no legal force or effect there can be no time limit within which to challenge the order or judgment. Further since the order has no legal force or effect, it can be repeatedly challenged, since no judge has the lawful authority to make a void order valid. Bates v. Board of Education, Allendale Community Consolidated School District No. 17, 136 Ill.2d 260, 267 (1990) (a court "cannot confer jurisdiction where none existed and cannot make a void proceeding valid."); People ex rel. Gowdy v. Baltimore & Ohio R.R. Co., 385 Ill. 86, 92, 52 N.E.2d 255 (1943).

## NO RESTRICTION ON VENUE TO VACATE A VOID ORDER

1. It is clear and well-established law that a void order can be challenged in any court. Old Wayne Mut. L.Assoc. v. McDonough, 204 U.S. 8, 27 S.Ct. 236 (1907) ("jurisdiction of any court exercising authority over a subject `may be inquired into in every other court when the proceedings in the former are relied upon and brought before the latter by a party claiming the benefit of such proceedings,' and the rule prevails whether `the decree or judgment has been given, in a court of admiralty, chancery, ecclesiastical court, or court of common law, or whether the point ruled has arisen under the laws of nations, the practice in chancery, or the municipal laws of states.'"); In re Marriage of Macino, 236 Ill.App.3d 886 (2nd Dist. 1992) ("if the order is void, it may be attacked at any time in any proceeding, "); Evans v. Corporate Services, 207 Ill.App.3d 297, 565N.E.2d 724 (2nd Dist. 1990) ("a void judgment, order or decree may be attacked at any time or in any court, either directly or collaterally"); Oak Park Nat. Bank v. Peoples Gas Light & Coke Co., 46 Ill.App.2d 385, 197 N.E.2d 73, 77 (1st Dist. 1964) ("that judgment is void and may be attacked at any time in the same or any other court, by the parties or by any other person who is affected thereby."). [Emphasis added].

## CAN BE CHALLENGED BY A THIRD PARTY

1. If an order or judgment was granted by a judge without subject-matter Jurisdiction in a court of limited jurisdiction, then a third-party to the action can challenge the validity of that order in any court, if the third party was damaged in any way by the void order. Since an order or judgment issued without subject-matter jurisdiction has no legal force or effect, it cannot be used to damage any other party. Oak Park Nat. Bank v. Peoples Gas Light & Coke Co., 46 Ill.App.2d 385, 197 N.E.2d 73, 77 (1st Dist. 1964) ("that judgment is void and may be attacked at any time in the same or any other court, by the parties or by any other person who is affected thereby."). [Emphasis added].

Acting Without Jurisdiction

## RCW 62A. 1-207 CODE

1. Some codes are very important, and should be embraced if you want to live in society. If you don't want to live a harmonious life, respecting other people, then you should go into the forest and live by yourself or with others who feel the way you do. However, if you do want to live in society, some codes are wonderful things. **SEE TWO WONDERFUL CODES ON PAGE 52.**

## Notice of Appreciation by The Real King Charles

1. The Real King Charles appreciates all the people who agree that they want to live together in harmony. So let's stop this fighting and confusion. Peace and knowledge is the only solution. The American people are not the problem. The government de facto and the greedy Money Powers of the World are the true problem. The government de facto wants all of the different races of people to constantly fight each other, while the government de facto robs the people blind of their Inalienable Rights, which are Freedom, Liberty, Property, and life. Some codes are wonderful, as long as they respect the people and are in line with The Constitutional Bill of Rights.

## IN COURT, YOU MUST HAVE THESE SEVEN ESSENTIAL ELEMENTS FOR A TRIAL

In Federal District Court, a claim must contain these seven (7) essential elements thereto be valid for a trial.

1. Accurate identification of the parties thereto the instrument, contract, or dispute.

2. Nature and content of the allegation or claim

3. Ledgering - accounting of the remedy or relief sought as recompense or compensation for the specific wrongs, contractual violations or defaults.

4. Evidence of solvency identification of the property sought/pledged as the take over of which the dispute occurs, thereto be forfeited thereto the prevailing party thereto pay the debt/damage and satisfy the judgment.

5. Facts and law specific laws violated, and facts set forth in evidence by exhibit.

6. Certification statement under oath by the party asserting an allegation or claim that everything asserted is "true, correct, and complete" whether criminal or civil.

7. Witness third party certification substantiating the legal identity of the party executing the instrument.

## THESE THREE ELEMENTS MUST BE PRESENT TO START A TORT CLAIM

1. There must be a mandatory duty.

2. The mandatory duty was breached.

3. Breach caused an injury.

**Initial request for a Tort Claim Number should be filed at the Risk Management Office, the Comptroller Office or who you intended to file your Tort Claim with.**

## ALL EXHIBITS MUST BE TITLED "AFFIDAVIT OF EXHIBITS" IN EVERY COURT THAT YOU FILE A CLAIM/COMPLAINT IN

REMEMBER THESE TWO WORDS - "**ADVERSE CLAIM.**" THESE WORDS ARE VERY IMPORTANT AND SHALL HELP YOU PROTECT YOUR PROPERTY IF YOU FILE A UCC1 FINANCING STATEMENT AGAINST YOUR DEBTOR AND THE PROPERTY OF THE DEBTOR.

## UNITED STATES CODE TITLE 18 USC § 1001

**1.** Whoever, in any matter within the Jurisdiction, of all departments or agencies of the United States, engages in any malicious concealment or cover ups by any trick, scheme, or device, a material fact; makes any maternally false, fictitious, or fraudulent statement or representation; or makes or uses any false writing or document knowing that it contains false, fictitious, or fraudulent statements or entries, shall be fined under this title or imprisoned not more than five years, or both.

## UNITED STATES CODE TITLE 18 USC § 242

### Deprivation of rights under color of law

**2.** Whoever, under color of any law, statute, ordinance, regulation, or custom, willfully subjects any person in any State, Territory, Commonwealth, Possession, or District to the deprivation of any rights, privileges, or immunities secured or protected by the Constitution or laws of the United States, or to different punishments, pains, or penalties, on account of such person being an alien or by reason of his color, or race, than are prescribed for the punishment of citizens, shall be fined under this title or imprisoned not more than one year, or both; and if bodily injury results from the acts committed in violation of this section or if such acts include the use, attempted use, or threatened use of a dangerous weapon, explosives, or fire, shall be fined under this title or imprisoned not more than ten years, or both; and if death results from the acts committed in violation of this section or if such acts include kidnapping or an attempt to kidnap, aggravated sexual abuse, or an attempt to commit aggravated sexual abuse, or an attempt to kill, shall be fined under this title, or imprisoned for any term of years or for life, or both, or may be sentenced to death.

## IF A COURT TRIES TO HAVE YOU EXAMINED BY TWO PSYCHIATRISTS IN AN ATTEMPT TO FORCE YOU TO USE AN ATTORNEY (SO THE COURT CAN HAVE JURISDICTION OVER PERSON)

1. One of the two psychiatrists is employed by the court and is going to say anything the court wants her or him to say. If you do not have your own psychiatrist, the government de facto is going to pay for a private

psychiatrist that they shall pick for you. Even if the other psychiatrist has a different diagnosis of your Mental Health, the court must hold a hearing to determine which psychiatrist is correct. Do you know what the magistrate's decision is going to be? Perhaps **Incapacitated!** It does not take a rocket scientist to determine what the court may try to make happen to you. You have got to be wise and refuse the examination. You must inform them that if they cannot prove jurisdiction over person, the law states that the case must be dismissed and no proceedings move forward.

2. If any psychiatrist tries to examine you, refuse. Do not answer any of their questions. Simply make this statement, **"No proceedings can move forward without my demand for proof of jurisdiction over person being proven to exist as a fact of the law." When asked, the court must prove that jurisdiction exists.**

3. If you are put in a room with a psychiatrist anywhere in the World, the only thing that you should say is, "I made a demand for proof of jurisdiction over person, to be proven to exist as a fact of the law. The law states, if any court fails to prove jurisdiction over person as a fact of the law, the case must be dismissed for lack of jurisdiction. If any magistrate proceeds with any further actions against you, it is considered a treasonable offense. If the officers of the court do not report the magistrate to the BAR for committing treason, and the magistrate is found guilty of treason, then the officers of the court that did not report the magistrate to the BAR for treason, may be guilty of treason as well."

4. A magistrate may still try to force you to use their Attorney, and if that happens to you while incarcerated, before you enter the government de facto courtroom you should say, "I am entering the government de facto courtroom **Under Duress**." When you are standing in front of the magistrate, you should also say these words: "**For the record, this person is not my Attorney and she or he does not represent me**." The magistrate may try to trick you again and ask, "So that means you are representing yourself?" Then you should say, "**If I represent myself, I shall be taking on the duties of an officer of the court and that shall make me liable to the court as well**. I am a government de jure American National, with full, unimpaired rights and standing in law and you are violating my Constitutional Rights."

## Notice of Acceptance of Constitutions Oath of Office
## For The United States Government Public Servants:

Public Servant: BRIAN HAN                    CERTIFIED MAIL: 7011 2000 8999 7766

dba: Magistrate In The New York City Criminal Court

County of New York

### *Point of Law*

For all contracts commence with an offer and is binding upon acceptance. See: "Contracts" by Farnsworth, third edition, sect. 3.3, pages 112,113.

The Federal Constitution of the United States and Constitution of the State of New York and the Oath of office as PUBLIC SERVANTS, amounts thereto nothing more than an offer that is an intention thereto act or refrain from acting in a specified way between <u>the respective</u> governments and <u>the Private</u> American People and for other purposes.

Be it known by those present that I, <u>Put Your Name Here</u>, am of the Natural Genealogy Heirs Lineal Descendants of the Native American Peoples of America Territories do hereby accept The Federal Constitution of the United States and Constitution of the State of New York and Oath of Office of the above named PUBLIC SERVANT as your open and binding offer thereof promise thereto form   <u>a firm</u> and binding contract between (1) The respective governments, and its political instrumentalities (2) The above named PUBLIC SERVANT (3) Myself in my Private Native American National Capacity.

I Reasonably Require that, as a PUBLIC SERVANT, you shall perform your promises and duties while staying in the limitations thereof Constitutions, creating no unfounded presumptions, Quasi Contracts nor Quasi In Rem Actions seeking only true facts and telling <u>the truth</u> at <u>all times</u> and respecting and protecting our secured rights thereof personal liberty and private property and <u>all rights</u> that is antecedent thereto.

For this Notice of Acceptance of Constitutions Oath of Office is made Ab initio explicitly without recourse and now constitutes for a "Binding Contract" and any deviation therefrom shall be treated as "Breach of Contract" "Breach of Fiduciary Duty of Performance" thereof and <u>a violation</u> thereof "Substantive Due Process".

### VERIFICATION
I, <u>Put Your Name Here</u>,  declare under penalty of perjury therein accordance with the laws of the united states of America that the foregoing is true, correct and complete to the best of one's knowledge and belief.

See: "Contracts" by Farnsworth, third edition, sect. 3.3, pages 112, 113

Offer and Acceptance; for the outward appearance of the agreement process, thereby which parties are satisfy by these requirements thereof bargain imposed by the doctrine of these consideration, varies wide according thereto circumstances. It may, for these examples, involve face-to-face negotiations, an exchange thereof letters or facsimiles, or may be <u>a perfunctory</u> signing of a printed form supplied thereby the other party, whatever for the outward appearance, it is common thereto analyze the process in terms of two distinct steps: first, <u>a manifestation</u> thereof assent that is called an *offer*, made by one party (the *offeror)* thereto another (the *offeree)*; and second, <u>a manifestation</u> thereof assent herein response that is called an *acceptance,*

Page   1 of 2

made by the offeree thereto <u>the offeror</u>. Although courts apply for this analysis on a case-by-case basis, depending on the circumstances, it gives <u>a reassuring</u> appearance thereof consistency.

What is an "offer"? It can be defined as <u>a manifestation</u> thereto another of the assent thereto enter into contract, if the other manifests assent <u>in return</u> by some action, often <u>a promise</u> but it is sometimes <u>a performance,</u> thereby making an offer. For the offeror thus confers on the offeree power thereto create <u>a contract</u>. An offer is nearly always <u>a promise</u> in a sense. For the action (promise or performance) which for the offeror presences conditions of the promise is for the "price" before it becomes enforceable. *Offer,* for the name given thereto <u>a promise</u> that is conditional on some action by the promisee *if* the legal effect thereof the promisee's taking that action. Therefor it is thereto make for the promise enforceable. Empowerment of the offeree thereto make for the offeror's promise enforceable is <u>the essence</u> of the offer. When does a promise empower for the promisee thereto take action that will make for the promise enforceable? In other words, when is <u>a manifestation</u> of the assent amount thereto an offer? For this is the main subject of this chapter.

What is an "acceptance"? It can be defined as an action (promise or performance) by the offeree that creates <u>a contract</u> that is (makes the offeror's promise enforceable). *Acceptance,* then, is the name given to the offeree's action if the legal effect of that action thereto makes offeror's promise enforceable. When does action by the promisee make for this promise enforceable? In other words, when does the promisee's action amount thereto an acceptance? This is another of the main subjects of this chapter.

Because of the requirement <u>of mutuality</u> <u>of obligation,</u> both parties are free thereto withdraw from negotiations until the moment when both are bound. For this moment is when the offeree accepts <u>the offer</u>. For the offeror is free to revoke such offer at any time before acceptance.

**Affidavit of Service**

Real King Charles is publishing these facts and has served the above Notice of Acceptance of Constitutions Oath of Office and Fiduciary Duty thereby mail or Hand Delivery, thereto <u>the following</u> men or women on the date below.]

Judicial Notice

SUBSCRIBED AND SWORN

THIS_____DAY

(New York State)

ss

(New York County)

_____ 2018

_____

    Notary Signature

Without Prejudice UCC 1-207
**Without Prejudice UCC 1-103**

Real King Charles _____
                      Autograph

Page 2 of 2

## IF ANYONE TRIES TO FILE A LAWSUIT AGAINST YOU AND THE PLAINTIFF'S ATTORNEY CALLED YOU TO TRY TO GET YOU TO SETTLE

1. When you talk to any Attorney on a telephone conference call, the first thing that you should ask is, "For the record, is this conversation being recorded?" Wait for her or his response! Then you should say, "Without Prejudice, all rights are reserved pertaining to the Constitution of the United States of America, [The Uniform Commercial Code, UCC 1-207 Anderson Version 1981 and UCC 1-103 Supplemental Principle of law]. I do not agree with any contract that is pertaining to this telephone conference call. I am participating in this conversation UNDER DURESS." Do not ever swear in over the telephone, and only swear in under duress.

## IF YOU EVER RECEIVE A SUMMONS

1. If you receive a summons from a ticket agent or police officer, the government de facto law gives you 48 hours to mail the summons in by Certified Mail. The author usually mails in the summons the same day, if possible. Sign your full name ----- ---- ---- and put "Authorized Representative" or "Agent" after your signature. Stamp over, through or alongside your signature Without Prejudice UCC 1-207 Anderson Version 1981. **Make a rubber stamp like the sample on page 26 of this Powerful Manual. "Do not ever plead."** If you do, you will be giving the magistrate jurisdiction over person and subject matter, and she or he will judge you. If you get an appearance letter from the court, you should write a Notice of Appearance to the magistrate. When you go to court, do not walk with any of the debtor IDs. If they ask you for your Driver's License, just say that you don't have one. All corporate IDs belong to the debtor, whose name is spelled in all capital letters. The debtors' name is on the Driver's License, and you are authorized to use the debtor property, but that is after you file a UCC1 FINANCIAL STATEMENT with the Secretary of State and gain control over all the debtor properties. Get a different Photo Identification card with your first, middle, and family names spelled in upper, lower case. Do not ever use initials in any part of your name. Always put "Without Prejudice UCC 1-207 Anderson Version 1981" on everything that you sign for the court, and make the court aware that you are there under duress. Also, make a demand for proof of jurisdiction over person to be proven to exist as a fact of law. The court does not have jurisdiction over a person just because you are in their courtroom. Follow the information in this Powerful Manual and do not let then con you.

Sample Photo Identification: Ben John Jackson
123 Park Avenue
New York, New York [10027]

# SEE SUMMONS AND LETTER FROM THE CRIMINAL COURT ON THE FOLLOWING PAGES

**SUMMONS**

423550872-6

The People of The State of New York VS.

Susp/Rev Check ☐ Yes   No ☐
Motorist Exhibited License   ☐ Yes   No ☐

| Last Name | | First Name | | M.I. |
|---|---|---|---|---|
| Street Address | | | Apt. No. | |
| City | | | State | Zip Code |
| ID Number | | Date of Birth | | Sex |
| Lic. State | Lic. Class or ID Type | Date Expires | | Operator Owns Vehicle ☐ Yes  No ☐ |

OPERATOR AND/OR OWNER OF VEHICLE BEARING LICENSE

| Plate No. | | NY CT PA NJ Other | | Reg. Expires |
|---|---|---|---|---|
| PAS OMT COM OML Other | | CHEV FORD HONDA DODG OLDS BUICK TOYT NISS Other | MO DAY YR | |
| SEDAN SUBN VAN TRUCK MCY Other | Veh. Yr. Veh. Color | Alternate Plate | State |

VIN No.

THE PERSON DESCRIBED ABOVE IS CHARGED AS FOLLOWS

| AM  PM  Time | Date of Offense | County | Precinct |
|---|---|---|---|
| ☐ ☐ | | | |

Place of Occurrence

IN VIOLATION OF

| | V.T.L. | Traff. Rules | Admin. Code | Penal Law | Other |
|---|---|---|---|---|---|
| Sec | Sub | | | | |

Description of Criminal Court Offense (including Traffic Misdemeanor)

| | SPEEDING | | DISOBEY TRAFF CONT DEV | Uninspec. Veh. | Unreg. Veh. | Unlic. Oper. |
|---|---|---|---|---|---|---|
| MPH | In MPH Zone | ☐ Sign | Pave ☐ Marks | Uninsur. Veh. | Com. Veh. | Bus  Haz. Mat. |
| | | ☐ Signal | | | | |

The person described above is summoned to appear at CRIMINAL COURT   Summons Part  County

Located at

Date of Appearance   9:30 a.m. _____ day of _____ year

I personally observed the commission of the offense charged above. False statements made herein are punishable as a Class A Misdemeanor pursuant to Section 210.45 of the Penal Law. Affirmed under penalty of perjury.

Rank/Full Signature of Complainant

Complainant's Full Name (printed)   Command Code

Agency/NCIC   Squad   Tax Registry No.

I acknowledge receipt of this summons. I understand it is my responsibility to read and comply with the instructions on my copy, and that my signature below is not an admission of guilt.

Without Prejudice UCC
Name

Without Prejudice UCC 1-207

CRIMINAL COURT

---

AA-500.2 (2/04)   CRIMINAL COURT – CITY OF NEW YORK

Failure to comply with these instructions may result in the issuance of a warrant for your arrest.

**TO PLEAD GUILTY**

YOU MUST PERSONALLY APPEAR AT THE COURT AND LOCATION SPECIFIED ON THE FACE OF THIS SUMMONS.

**TO PLEAD NOT GUILTY**

By Mail:
Within 48 hours after receipt of this summons complete the PLEA FORM below and mail this summons to the NOT GUILTY UNIT at the Court and location specified on the face of this summons. The Court will then notify you by mail of the date to appear for trial. If you do not hear from the Court within 30 days after the return date, APPEAR IN PERSON.

In Person:
Appear in person or by counsel on the date and time set for appearance at the Court and location specified on the face of this Summons. A second court appearance will then be required at a later date for trial.

UPON APPEARING FOR ARRAIGNMENT - YOU HAVE THE RIGHT

To the aid of counsel at your arraignment and at every subsequent stage of the action.

To an adjournment for the purpose of obtaining counsel.

To have counsel assigned by the Court if you are financially unable to obtain counsel except if you are charged with a traffic infraction.

To have a supporting deposition filed as provided in section 100.25 of the Criminal Procedure Law when the accusatory instrument filed against you is a Simplified Information.

IF TRAFFIC OFFENSE OTHER THAN PARKING OR JAYWALKING IS CHARGED: A plea of guilty to this charge is equivalent to a conviction after trial. If you are convicted, not only will you be liable to a penalty, but in addition your license to drive a motor vehicle or motorcycle, and your certificate of registration, if any, are subject to suspension and revocation as prescribed by law.

DO NOT DETACH. SUBMIT ENTIRE SUMMONS.

PLEA FORM

I hereby plead not guilty   Without Prejudice UCC 1-207

| NAME (Print) | |
|---|---|
| ADDRESS | |
| CITY | STATE  ZIP CODE |
| SIGNATURE | DATE |

Do not ever use UCC 1-308

**SUMMONS**

23558771-7

The People of The State of New York VS.

Susp/Rev Check ☐ Yes No ☐
Motorist Exhibited License ☐ Yes No ☐

Last Name _____ First Name *Charles* M.I.

Str MADISON Ave Apt. No.

City New York State NY Zip Code 10035

ID Number 307 556 530 Date of Birth 12-22-58 Sex M

Lic. State NY Lic. Class of ID Type Date Expires 12-22-11 Operator Owns Vehicle ☐ Yes No ☐

**OPERATOR AND/OR OWNER OF VEHICLE BEARING LICENSE**

Plate No. ... NY CT PA NJ Other ... Reg. Expires

VIN No.

**THE PERSON DESCRIBED ABOVE IS CHARGED AS FOLLOWS**

Time 12:00 Date of Offense 12-18-04 County NY Precinct

Place of Occurrence

IN VIOLATION OF 210.70.5

Sec. 210.70 Sub 5

Description of Criminal Court Offense (including Traffic Misdemeanor)

Black ...

The person described above is summoned to appear at CRIMINAL COURT

Located at 346 P. M.

Date of Appearance 9:30 a.m. 14 day of 3 year

I personally observed the commission of the offense charged above. False statements made herein are punishable as a Class A Misdemeanor pursuant to Section 210.45 of the Penal Law. Affirmed under penalty of perjury.

Rank/Full Signature of Complainant

Complainant's Full Name (printed)

Agency/NCIC

I acknowledge receipt of this summons. I understand it is my responsibility to read and comply with the instructions on my copy, and that my signature below is not an admission of guilt.

*Without Prejudice UCC 1-207*

Name *Charles* agent Date 12-18-04

*Without Prejudice UCC '*

**CRIMINAL COURT**

---

AA-500.2 (2/04)    CRIMINAL COURT – CITY OF NEW YORK

Failure to comply with these instructions may result in the issuance of a warrant for your arrest.

TO PLEAD GUILTY

YOU MUST PERSONALLY APPEAR AT THE COURT AND LOCATION SPECIFIED ON THE FACE OF THIS SUMMONS.

TO PLEAD NOT GUILTY

By Mail:
Within 48 hours after receipt of this summons complete the PLEA FORM below and mail this summons to the NOT GUILTY UNIT at the Court and location specified on the face of this summons. The Court will then notify you by mail of the date to appear for trial. If you do not hear from the Court within 30 days after the return date, APPEAR IN PERSON.

In Person:
Appear in person or by counsel on the date and time set for appearance at the Court and location specified on the face of this Summons. A second court appearance will then be required at a later date for trial.

UPON APPEARING FOR ARRAIGNMENT – YOU HAVE THE RIGHT

To the aid of counsel at your arraignment and at every subsequent stage of the action.

To an adjournment for the purpose of obtaining counsel.

To have counsel assigned by the Court if you are financially unable to obtain counsel except if you are charged with a traffic infraction.

To have a supporting deposition filed as provided in section 100.25 of the Criminal Procedure Law when the accusatory instrument filed against you is a Simplified Information.

IF TRAFFIC OFFENSE OTHER THAN PARKING OR JAYWALKING IS CHARGED: A plea of guilty to this charge is equivalent to a conviction after trial. If you are convicted, not only will you be liable to a penalty, but in addition your license to drive a motor vehicle or motorcycle, and your certificate of registration, if any, are subject to suspension and revocation as prescribed by law.

DO NOT DETACH. SUBMIT ENTIRE SUMMONS.

**PLEA FORM**

I hereby plead not guilty

NAME (Print) *Without Prejudice UCC 1-308* / *Without Prejudice UCC 1-207*

ADDRESS

CITY    STATE    ZIP CODE

SIGNATURE    DATE

---

Do not ever use UCC 1-308

AA-500.2 (2/04)

**SUMMONS**

**423558770-5**

The People of The State of New York VS.

Susp/Rev Check ☐ Yes  No ☐
Motorist Exhibited License  ☐ Yes  No ☐

Last Name ___ Cibates  First Name ___ M.I.

Street Address ___ MADISON AVE  Apt. N ___

City ___ New York  State NU  Zip Code 10035

ID Number 351 556 530  Date of Birth 12-22-58  Sex M

Lic. State NU  Lic. Class or ID Type B  Date Expires 12-22-11  Operator Owns Vehicle ☐ Yes  No ☐

Plate No. ___

OPERATOR AND/OR OWNER OF VEHICLE BEARING LICENSE

THE PERSON DESCRIBED ABOVE IS CHARGED AS FOLLOWS

AM ☐ Time 1700 PM ☐  Date of Offense 12/18/04  County NU  Precinct

Place of Occurrence 11 W125 ST + 771E

IN VIOLATION OF
Sec 210 20.2 Sub

Description of Criminal Court Offense (Including Traffic Misdemeanor)
Unreasonable Noise

The person described above is summoned to appear at CRIMINAL COURT
Located at 346 Bromy  Summons Part 157  County NU

Date of Appearance 9:30 a.m.  14 day of 03 year 05

I personally observed the commission of the offense charged above. False statements made herein are punishable as a Class A Misdemeanor pursuant to Section 210.45 of the Penal Law. Affirmed under penalty of perjury.

Rank/Full Signature of Complainant

Complainant's Full Name (printed)  Command Code

Agency/INQRC  Squad  Tax Registry No.

I acknowledge receipt of this summons. I understand it is my responsibility to read and comply with the instructions on my copy, and that my signature below is not an admission of guilt.

Without Prejudice UCC 1-207

Name _Chank_  agent  Date 12-18-04

Without Prejudice UCC

**CRIMINAL COURT**

---

AA-500.2 (2/04)

**CRIMINAL COURT – CITY OF NEW YORK**

Failure to comply with these instructions may result in the issuance of a warrant for your arrest.

<u>TO PLEAD GUILTY</u>

YOU MUST PERSONALLY APPEAR AT THE COURT AND LOCATION SPECIFIED ON THE FACE OF THIS SUMMONS.

<u>TO PLEAD NOT GUILTY</u>

By Mail:

Within 48 hours after receipt of this summons complete the PLEA FORM below and mail this summons to the NOT GUILTY UNIT at the Court and location specified on the face of this summons. The Court will then notify you by mail of the date to appear for trial. If you do not hear from the Court within 30 days after the return date, APPEAR IN PERSON.

In Person:

Appear in person or by counsel on the date and time set for appearance at the Court and location specified on the face of this Summons. A second court appearance will then be required at a later date for trial.

**UPON APPEARING FOR ARRAIGNMENT – <u>YOU HAVE THE RIGHT</u>**

To the aid of counsel at your arraignment and at every subsequent stage of the action.

To an adjournment for the purpose of obtaining counsel.

To have counsel assigned by the Court if you are financially unable to obtain counsel <u>except</u> if you are charged with a traffic infraction.

To have a supporting deposition filed as provided in section 100.25 of the Criminal Procedure Law <u>when</u> the accusatory instrument filed against you is a Simplified Information.

IF TRAFFIC OFFENSE OTHER THAN PARKING OR JAYWALKING IS CHARGED: A plea of guilty to this charge is equivalent to a conviction after trial. If you are convicted, not only will you be liable to a penalty, but in addition your license to drive a motor vehicle or motorcycle, and your certificate of registration, if any, are subject to suspension and revocation as prescribed by law.

DO NOT DETACH. SUBMIT ENTIRE SUMMONS.

| PLEA FORM |
|---|
| I hereby plead not guilty |
| NAME (Print) ~~Without Prejudice UCC 1-308~~ Without Prejudice UCC 1-207 |
| ADDRESS |
| CITY  STATE  ZIP CODE |
| SIGNATURE  DATE |

**Do not ever use UCC 1-308**

CRIMINAL COURT OF THE CITY OF NEW YORK
COUNTY OF NEW YORK

CHARLES
    MADISON
NEW YORK, NY  10035-2760

The case(s) referenced below was dismissed on 01/26/2005 in Part SAP-D and was
sealed pursuant to Section 160.50 CPL.

No appearance in court is required regarding this matter.  Retain this notice for your records.

| Summons Number | Date Issued | Docket Number |
| --- | --- | --- |
| 42355̈ | 12/18/200 | 2005SNC |
| 423556 | 12/18/20 | 2005SN0 |

CRIMINAL COURT OF THE CITY OF NEW YORK
COUNTY OF NEW YORK
346 BROADWAY
NEW YORK, NY  10013

CHARLES
    ADISON A
NEW YORK, NY  10035-2760

10035+2760

CRIMINAL COURT OF THE CITY OF NEW YORK
COUNTY OF NEW YORK

CHARLES

NEW YORK, NY 10033

The case(s) referenced below was dismissed on 04/19/2005 in Part SAP-D and was sealed pursuant to Section 160.50 CPL.

No appearance in court is required regarding this matter. Retain this notice for your records.

| Summons Number | Date Issued | Docket Number |
|---|---|---|
| 42° | 03/1 | 200 |

CRIMINAL COURT OF THE CITY OF NEW YORK
COUNTY OF NEW YORK
346 BROADWAY
NEW YORK NY 10013

CHARLES

NEW YORK, NY 10033

## ALL OF THE CHURCHES IN AMERICA LOST THEIR SOVEREIGNTY

1. The government de facto trickery has caused many churches to shut their doors, church after church. Some government de facto corporations got people of the churches to sign fraudulent Corporate Contracts that offered them the world, but at the end of the day, left them without a church. There are very few churches that are standing on holy ground. The Real King Charles is offering the churches their freedom from the Corporate United States. This is the churches' opportunity to stand up and say, "NO! WE DO NOT WANT TO DO ANY MORE BUSINESS WITH THE CORPORATE GOVERNMENT DE FACTO. We are standing with our Creator, the Bible, the Constitution of the United States of America and the Uniform Commercial Code. The churches possess the right to back out of any government de facto fraudulent Contract." The people are the church and shall always be the church. The Constitution of the United States of America guarantees the separation of church and state. The Temple is also a religious building. One person alone cannot sell a Temple because a church is more than one person. Roughly around 1952, the government de facto creeped into the churches, and tricked the churches into becoming a corporation. I am demanding that the government de facto cease and desist of all acts against any church that chooses to break free from the corporate government de facto.

2. This **Powerful Manual** is completed for now. Please remember the meaning of life, which is to "live and do right."

# The Constitution
## of the
# United States of America

We the People of the United States, in Order to form a more perfect Union, establish Justice insure domestic Tranquility, provide for the common defence, promote the general Welfare, and secure the Blessings of Liberty to ourselves and our Posterity, do ordain and establish this Constitution for the United States of America.

## Article I

**Section 1** ◦ All legislative Powers herein granted shall be vested in a Congress of the United States, which shall consist of a Senate and House of Representatives.

**Section 2** ◦ The House of Representatives shall be composed of Members chosen every second Year by the People of the several States, and the Electors in each State shall have the Qualifications requisite for Electors of the most numerous Branch of the State Legislature.

No Person shall be a Representative who shall not have attained to the age of twenty five Years, and been seven Years a Citizen of the United States, and who shall not, when elected, be an Inhabitant of that State in which he shall be chosen. *Representatives and Direct Taxes shall be apportioned among the several States which may be included within this Union, according to their respective Numbers. which shall be determined by adding to the whole Number of free Persons, including those bound to Service for a Term of Years, and excluding Indians not taxed, three fifths of all other persons.* * The actual Enumeration shall be made within three Years after the first Meeting of the Congress of the United States, and within every subsequent Term of ten Years, in such Manner as they shall by Law direct. The Number of Representatives shall not exceed one for every thirty Thousand, but each State shall have at Least one Representative; and until such enumeration shall be made, the State of New Hampshire shall be entitled to chuse

three, Massachusetts eight, Rhode-Island and Providence Plantations one, Connecticut five, New-York six, New Jersey four, Pennsylvania eight, Delaware one, Maryland six, Virginia ten, North Carolina five, South Carolina five, and Georgia three.

When vacancies happen in the Representation from any State, the Executive Authority thereof shall issue Writs of Election to fill such Vacancies.

The House of Representatives shall chuse their Speaker and other Officers; and shall have the sole Power of Impeachment.

**Section 3** ◦ The Senate of the United States shall be composed of two Senators from each State, chosen by the Legislature thereof, ‡ for six Years; and each Senator shall have one Vote.

Immediately after they shall be assembled in Consequence of the first Election, they shall be divided as equally as may be into three Classes. The Seats of the Senators of the first Class shall be vacated at the Expiration of the second Year, of the Second class at the Expiration of the fourth Year, and of the third Class at the Expiration of the sixth Year, so that one third may be chosen every second Year; and if vacancies happen by Resignation, or otherwise during the Recess of the Legislature of any State, the Executive thereof may make temporary Appointments until the next Meeting of the Legislature, which shall then fill such Vacancies. †

No Person shall be a Senator who shall not have attained to the Age of thirty Years, and been nine Years a Citizen of the United States, and who shall not, when elected, be an Inhabitant of the State for which he shall be chosen.

The Vice President of the United States shall be President of the Senate, but shall have no Vote, unless they be equally divided.

The Senate shall chuse their other Officers, and also a President pro tempore, in the Absence of the Vice President, or when he shall exercise the Office of President of the United States.

The Senate shall have the sole Power to try all Impeachments. When sitting for that Purpose, they shall be on Oath or Affirmation. When the President of the United States is tried, the Chief Justice shall preside: And no Peon shall be convicted without the Concurrence of two thirds of the Members present.

Judgment in Cases of Impeachment shall not extend further than to removal from Office, and disqualification to hold and enjoy any Office of honor, Trust or Profit under the United States: but the Party convicted shall nevertheless be liable and subject to Indictment, Trial, Judgment and Punishment, according to Law.

* Italics indicate passages altered by later amendments. This was revised by the Sixteenth (apportionment of taxes) and Fourteenth (determination of persons) amendments.
‡ Revised by Seventeenth Amendment.
† Revised by Seventeenth Amendment.

**Section 4** • The Times, Place and Manner of holding Elections for Senators and Representatives, shall be prescribed in each State by the Legislature thereof; but the Congress may at any time by Law make or alter such Regulations, except as to the Places of chusing Senators.

The Congress shall assemble at least once in every Year, and such Meeting shall be on the first Monday in December, ‡ unless they shall by Law appoint a different Day.

**Section 5** • Each House shall be the Judge of the Elections, Returns and Qualifications of its own Members, and a Majority of each shall constitute a Quorum to do Business; but a smaller Number may adjourn from day to day, and may be authorized to compel the Attendance of absent Members, in such Manner, and under such Penalty as each House may provide.

Each House may determine the Rules of its Proceedings, punish its Members for disorderly Behavior, and, with the Concurrence of two thirds expel a Member.

Each House shall keep a journal of its Proceedings, and from time to time publish the same, excepting such Parts as may in their Judgment require Secrecy; and the Yeas and Nays of the Members of either House on any question shall, at the Desire of one fifth of those Present, be entered on the Journal.

Neither House, during the Session of Congress, shall, without the Consent of the other, adjourn for more than three days. nor to any other Place than that in which the two Houses shall be Sitting.

**Section 6** • The Senators and Representatives shall receive a Compensation for their Services, to be ascertained by Law, and paid out of the Treasury of the United States. They shall in all Cases, except Treason, Felony and Breach of the Peace, be privileged from Arrest during their Attendance at the Session of their respective Houses, and in going to and returning from the same; and for any Speech or Debate in either House, they shall not be questioned in any other Place.

No Senator or Representative shall, during the Time for which he was elected, be appointed to any civil Office under the Authority of the United States, which shall have been created, or the Emoluments whereof shall have been encreased during such time; and no Person holding any Office under the United States, shall be a Member of either House during his Continuance in Office.

**Section 7** • All Bills for raising Revenue shall originate in the house of Representatives; but the Senate may propose or concur with Amendments as on other Bills.

Every Bill which shall have passed the House of Representatives and the Senate, shall, before it become a Law, be presented to the President of the United States; if he approve he shall sign it, but if not he shall return it, with his Objections to that House in which it shall have originated, who shall enter the Objections at large on their Journal, and proceed to reconsider it. If after such Reconsideration two thirds of that House shall agree to pass the Bill, it shall be sent, together with the Objections, to the other House, by which it shall likewise be reconsidered, and if approved by two thirds of that House, it shall become a Law. But in all such Cases the Votes of both Houses shall be determined by Yeas and Nays, and the Names of the Persons voting for and against the Bill shall be entered on the Journal of each House respectively. If any Bill shall not be returned by the President within ten Days (Sundays excepted) after it shall have been presented to him, the Same shall be a Law, in like Manner as if he had signed it, unless the Congress by their Adjournment prevent its Return, in which Case it shall not be a Law.

Every Order, Resolution, or Vote to which the Concurrence of the Senate and House of Representatives may be necessary (except on a question of Adjournment) shall be presented to the President of the United States; and before the Same shall take Effect, shall be approved by him, or being disapproved by him, shall·be repassed by two thirds of the Senate and House of Representatives, according to the Rules and Limitations prescribed in the Case of a Bill.

**Section 8** • The Congress shall have Power To lay and collect Taxes, Duties, Imposts and Excises, to pay the Debts and provide for the common Defence and general Welfare of the United States; but all Duties, Imposts and Excises **shall be uniform throughout the United States;** ___

To borrow Money on the credit of the United States;

To regulate Commerce with foreign Nations, and among the several States, and with the Indian Tribes;

To establish an uniform Rule of Naturalization, and uniform Laws on the subject of Bankruptcies throughout the United States;

‡ Revised by Twentieth Amendment.

To coin Money, regulate the Value thereof, and of foreign Coin, and fix the Standard of Weights and Measure;

To provide for the Punishment of counterfeiting the Securities and current Coin of the United States;

To establish Post Offices and post Roads;

To promote the Progress of Science and useful Arts, by securing for limited Times to Authors and Inventors the exclusive Right to their respective Writings and Discoveries; To constitute Tribunals inferior to the Supreme Court;

To define and punish piracies and Felonies committed on the high Seas, and Offences against the Law of Nations;

To declare War, grant Letters of Marque and Reprisal, and make Rules concerning Captures on Land and Water;

To raise and support Armies, but no Appropriation of Money to that Use shall be for a longer Term than two Years;

To provide and maintain a Navy;

To make Rules for the Government and Regulation of the land and naval Forces;

To provide for calling forth the Militia to execute the Laws of the Union, suppress Insurrections and repel Invasions;

To provide for organizing, arming, and disciplining. the Militia, and for governing such Part of them as may be employed in the Service of the United States, reserving to the States respectively, the Appointment of the Officers, and the Authority of training the Militia according to the discipline prescribed by Congress;

To exercise exclusive Legislation in all Cases whatsoever, over such District (not exceeding ten Mile square) as may, by Cession of particular States, and the Acceptance of Congress, become the Seat of the Government of the United States, and to exercise like Authority over all Places purchased by the Consent of the Legislature of the State in which the Same shall be, for the Erection of Forts, Magazines, Arsenals, dock-Yards, and other needful Buildings;

—And

To make all Laws which shall be necessary and proper for carrying into Execution the foregoing Powers, and all other Powers vested by this Constitution in the Government of the United State, or in any Department or Office thereof.

Section 9 • The Migration or Importation of such Persons as any of the States now existing shall think proper to admit, shall not be prohibited by the Congress prior to the Year one thousand eight hundred and eight, but a Tax or duty may be imposed on such Importation, not exceeding ten dollars for each Person.

The Privilege of the Writ of Habeas Corpus shall not be suspended, unless when in Cases of Rebellion or Invasion the public Safety may require it.

No Bill of Attainder or ex post facto Law shall be passed.

No Capitation, or other direct, Tax shall be laid, unless in Proportion to the Census or Enumeration herein before directed to be taken. *

No Tax or Duty shall be laid on Articles exported from any State.

No Preference shall be given by any Regulation of Commerce or Revenue to the Ports of one State over those of another: nor shall Vessels bound to, or from, one State, be obliged to enter, clear, or pay Duties in another.

No Money shall be drawn from the Treasury, but in Consequence of Appropriations made by Law; and a regular Statement and Account of the Receipts and Expenditures of all public Money shall be published from time to time.

No title of Nobility shall be granted by the United States: And no Person holding any Office of Profit or Trust under them, shall, without the Consent of the Congress, accept of any present, Emolument, Office, or Title, of any kind whatever, from any King, Prince, or foreign State.

Section 10 • No State shall enter into any Treaty, Alliance, or Confederation; grant Letters of Marque and Reprisal; coin Money; emit Bills of Credit; make any Thing but gold and silver coin a Tender in Payment of Debts; pass any Bill of Attainder, ex post facto Law, or Law impairing the Obligation of Contracts, or Grant any Title of Nobility.

* Revised by Sixteenth Amendment.

The Only Way Out

No State shall, without the Consent of the Congress, lay any Imposts or Duties on Imports or Exports, except what may be absolutely necessary for executing its inspection Laws: and the net Produce of all Duties and Imposts, laid by any State on Imports or Exports, shall be for the Use of the Treasury of the United States; and all such Laws shall be subject to the Revision and Control of the Congress.

No State shall, without the Consent of Congress, lay any Duty of Tonnage, keep Troops, or Ships of War in time of Peace, enter into any Agreement or Compact with another Stare, or with a foreign Power, or engage in War, unless actually invaded, or in such imminent Danger as will not admit of delay.

## Article II

Section 1 • The executive Power shall be vested in a President of the United States of America. He shall hold his Office during the Term of four Years, † and, together with the Vice President, chosen for the same Term be elected as follows:

Each State shall appoint, in such Manner as the Legislature thereof may direct, a Number of Electors, equal to the whole Number of Senators and Representatives to which the State may be entitled in the Congress but no Senator or Representative, or Person holding an Office of Trust or Profit under the United States, shall be appointed an Elector.

The Electors shall meet in their respective States, and vote by Ballot for two Persons, of whom one at least shall not be an Inhabitant of the some State with themselves And they shall make a List of all the Persons voted for, and of the

Number of Votes for each; which List they shall sign and certify, and transmit sealed to the Seat of the Government of the United States directed to the President of the Senate. President of the Senate shall in the Presence of the Senate and House of Representatives open all the Certificates and the Votes shall then be counted. The

Person having the greatest Number of Votes shall be the President, if such Number

be a Majority of the whole Number of Electors appointed; and if there be more than one who have such Majority, and have an equal Number of Votes then the House of Representatives shall immediately chuse by Ballot one of them for President; and if no Person have a Majority, then from the five highest on the List the said House shall in like Manner chuse the President. But in chusing the President, the Votes shall be taken by States the Representation from each State having one Vote; A quorum for this purpose shall consist of a Member or Members from two thirds of the States and a Majority of all the States shall be necessary to a Choice. In every

Case, after the Choice of the President, the Person having the greatest Number of Votes of the Electors shall be the Vice President. But if there should remain two or more who have equal votes the Senate shall chuse from them by Ballot the Vice President. *

The Congress may determine the Time of chusing the Electors, and the Day on which they shall give their Votes; which Day shall be the same throughout the United States.

No Person except a natural born Citizen, or a Citizen of the United States, at the time of the Adoption of this Constitution, shall be eligible to the Office of President; neither shall any Person be eligible to that Office who shall not have attained to the Age of thirty five Years, and been fourteen Years a Resident within the United States.

In case of the Removal of the President from Office, or of his Death, Resignation, or Inability to discharge the Powers and Duties of the said Office, the Some shall devolve on the Vice President, and the Congress may by Law provide for the Case of Removal, Death, Resignation or Inability, both of the President and Vice President, declaring what Officer shall then act as President, and such Officer shall act accordingly, until the Disability be removed, or a President shall be elected. ‡

The President shall, at stated Times, receive for his Services, a Compensation which shall neither be encreased nor diminished during the Period for which he shall have been elected, and he shall not receive within that Period any other Emolument from the United States, or any of them.

† See Twenty-second Amendment.
* Superseded by Twelfth Amendment.
‡ Revised by Twenty-fifth Amendment.

Before he enter on the Execution of his Office, he shall take the following Oath or Affirmation:—"I do solemnly swear (or affirm) that I will faithfully execute the Office of President of the United States, and will to the best of my Ability, preserve, protect and defend the Constitution of the United States.

Section 2 • The President shall be Commander in Chief of the Army and Navy of the United States, and of the Militia of the several States, when called into the actual service of the United States; he may require the Opinion, in writing, of the principal Officer in each of the executive Departments, upon any Subject relating to the Duties of their respective Offices, and he shall have Power to grant Reprieve and Pardons for Offences against the United States, except in Cases of Impeachment.

He shall have Power, by and with the Advice and Consent of the Senate, to make Treaties, provided two thirds of the Senators present concur; and he shall nominate, and by and with the Advice and Consent of the Senate, shall appoint Ambassadors, and other public Ministers and Consuls, Judges of the supreme Court, and all other Officers of the United States, whose Appointments are not herein otherwise provided for, and which shall be established by Law: but the Congress may by Law Vest the Appointment of such inferior Officers, as they think proper, in the President alone, in the Courts of Law, or in the Heads of Departments.

The President shall have Power to fill up all Vacancies that may happen during the Recess of the Senate, by granting Commissions which shall expire at the End of their next Session.

Section 3 • He shall from time to time give to the Congress Information of the State of the Union, and recommend to their Consideration such Measures as he shall judge necessary and expedient; he may, on extraordinary Occasions, convene both Houses, or either of them, and in Case of Disagreement between them, with respect to the Time of Adjournment, he may adjourn them to such Time as he shall think proper; he shall receive Ambassadors and other public Ministers, he shall take Care that the Laws be faithfully executed, and shall Commission all the Officers of the United States.

Section 4 • The President, Vice President, and all civil Officers of the United States, shall be removed from Office on Impeachment for, and Conviction of Treason, Bribery, or other high Crimes and Misdemeanors.

### Article III

Section 1 • The judicial Power of the United States, shall be vested in one supreme Court and in such inferior Courts as the Congress may from time to time ordain and establish. The Judges both of the supreme and inferior Courts, shall hold their Office during good Behavior, and shall, at stated Time, receive for their Services, a Compensation, which shall not be diminished during their Continuance in Office.

Section 2 • The judicial Power shall extend to all Cases in Law and Equity, arising under this Constitution, the Laws of the United States, and Treaties made, or which shall be made, under their Authority;—to all Cases affecting Ambassadors, other public Ministers and Consuls;—to all Cases of admiralty and maritime Jurisdiction; —to Controversies to which the United States shall be a party;—to Controversies between two or more States;—between a State and Citizens of another State;—between Citizens of different State;—between Citizens of the same State claiming Lands under Grants of different states and between a State or the Citizens thereof, and foreign States, Citizens, or Subjects. *

In all cases affecting Ambassadors, other public Ministers and Consuls, and those in which a State shall be party, the supreme Court shall have original Jurisdiction. In all the other Cases before mentioned, the supreme Court shall have appellate Jurisdiction, both as to Law and Fact, with such Exceptions, and under such Regulations as the Congress shall make.

The Trial of all Crimes, except in Cases of Impeachment, shall be by Jury; and such Trial shall be held in the State where the said Crimes shall have been committed; but when not committed within any State, the Trial shall be at such Place or Places as the Congress may by Law have directed.

*Revised by Eleventh Amendment.

**Section 3 •** Treason against the United States, shall consist only in levying War against them, or in adhering to their Enemies, giving them Aid and Comfort. No Person shall be convicted of Treason unless on the Testimony of two Witnesses to the same overt Act, or on Confession in open Court.

The Congress shall have Power to declare the Punishment of Treason, but no Attainder of Treason shall work Corruption of Blood, or Forfeiture except during the Life of the Person attained.

## Article IV

**Section 1 •** Full Faith and Credit shall be given in each State to the public Acts, Records, and judicial Proceedings of every other State. And the Congress may by general Laws prescribe the Manner in which such Acts, Records and Proceedings shall be proved, and the Effect thereof.

**Section 2 •** The Citizens of each State shall be entitled to all Privileges and Immunities of Citizens in the several States.

A Person charged in any State with Treason, Felony, or other Crime, who shall flee from Justice, and be found in another State, shall on Demand of the executive Authority of the State from which he fled, be delivered up, to be removed to the State having Jurisdiction of the Crime.

No person held to service or Labour in one State, under the Laws thereof, escaping into another, shall, in Consequence of any Law or Regulation therein, be discharged from such service or Labour, but shall be delivered up on Claim of the party to whom such service or Labour may be due.†

**Section 3 •** New States may be admitted by the Congress into this Union; but no new State shall be formed or erected within the Jurisdiction of any other State; nor any State be formed by the Junction of two or more States, or Parts of States, without the Consent of the Legislatures of the States concerned as well as of the Congress.

The Congress shall have Power to dispose of and make all needful Rules and Regulations respecting the Territory or other Property belonging to the United States; and nothing in this Constitution shall be so construed as to Prejudice any claims of the United States, or of any particular State.

**Section 4 •** The United States shall guarantee to every State in this Union a Republican Form of Government, and shall protect each of them against Invasion; and on Application of the Legislature, or of the Executive (when the Legislature cannot be convened) against domestic Violence.

## Article V

The Congress, whenever two thirds of both Houses shall deem it necessary, shall propose Amendments to this Constitution, or, on the Application of the Legislatures of two thirds of the several States, shall call a Convention for proposing Amendments, which, in either Case, shall be valid to all Intents and Purposes, as Part of this Constitution, when ratified by the Legislatures of three fourths of the several States, or by Conventions in three fourths thereof, as the one or the other Mode of Ratification may be proposed by the Congress; Provided that no Amendment which may be made prior to the Year One thousand eight hundred and eight shall in any Manner affect the first and fourth Clauses in the Ninth Section of the first Article; and that no State. without its Consent, shall be deprived of its equal Suffrage in the Senate.

## Article VI

All Debts contracted and Engagements entered into, before the Adoption of this Constitution, shall be as valid against the United States under this Constitution as under the Confederation. *

This Constitution, and the Laws of the United States which shall be made in Pursuance thereof; and all Treaties made, or which shall be made, under the Authority of the United States shall be the supreme Law of the Land; and the Judges in every State shall be bound thereby, any Thing in the Constitution or Laws of any State to the Contrary notwithstanding.

† Superseded by Thirteenth Amendment.
* See Fourteenth Amendment, Section 4.

The Senators and Representatives before mentioned, and the Members of the several State Legislatures, and all executive and judicial Officers, both of the United States and of the several States shall be bound by Oath or Affirmation to support this Constitution; but no religious Test shall ever be required as a Qualification to any Office or public Trust under the United States.

### Article VII

The Ratification of the Conventions of nine States shall be sufficient for the Establishment of this Constitution between the States so ratifying the Same.

Done in Convention by the Unanimous Consent of the States present the Seventeenth Day of September in the Year of our Lord one thousand seven hundred and eighty seven and of the Independence of the United States of America the twelfth. In witness whereof We have hereunto subscribed our Names.

# The Bill of Rights

## The First Ten (10) Admedments are called the Bill of Rights

ARTICLES IN ADDITION TO, AND AMENDMENT OF, THE CONSTITUTION OF THE UNITED STATES OF AMERICA, PROPOSED BY CONGRESS, AND RATIFIED BY THE SEVERAL STATES, PURSUANT TO THE FIFTH ARTICLE OF THE ORIGINAL CONSTITUTION.
(Ratification of the first ten amendments was completed December 15, 1791.)

### Amendment I

Congress shall make no law respecting an establishment of religion, or prohibiting the free exercise thereof; or abridging the freedom of speech, or of the press, or the right of the people peaceably to assemble, and to petition the Government for a redress of grievances.

### Amendment II

A well regulated Militia, being necessary to the security of a free State, the right of the people to keep and bear Arms, shall not be infringed.

### Amendment III

No Soldier shall, in time of peace be quartered in any house, without the consent of the Owner, nor in time of war, but in a manner to be prescribed by law.

### Amendment IV ✔

The right of the people to be secure in their persons, houses, papers, and effects, against unreasonable searches and seizures, shall not be violated, and no Warrants shall issue, but upon probable cause, supported by Oath or affirmation, and particularly describing the place to be searched, and the persons or things to be seized.

### Amendment V

No person shall be held to answer for a capital, or other infamous crime, unless on a presentment or indictment of a Grand Jury, except in cases arising in the land or naval forces, or in the Militia, when in actual service in time of War or public danger; nor shall any person be subject for the same offence to be twice put in jeopardy of life or limb; nor shall be compelled in any criminal case to be a witness against himself, nor be deprived of life, liberty, or property, without due process of law; nor shall private property be taken for public use, without just compensation.

### Amendment VI

In all criminal prosecutions the accused shall enjoy the right to a speedy and public trial, by an impartial jury of the State and district wherein the crime shall have been committed, which district shall have been previously ascertained by law, and to be informed of the nature and cause of the accusation; to be confronted with the witnesses against him to have compulsory process for obtaining witnesses in his favor, and to have the Assistance of Counsel for his defence.

### Amendment VII

In Suits at common law, where the value in controversy shall exceed twenty dollars, the right of trial by jury shall be preserved, and no fact tried by a jury, shall be otherwise reexamined in any Court of the United States than according to the rules of the common law.

### Amendment VIII

Excessive bail shall not be required, nor excessive fines imposed, nor cruel and unusual punishments inflicted.

### Amendment IX

The enumeration in the Constitution, of certain rights, shall not be construed to deny or disparage others retained by the people.

### Amendment X

The powers not delegated to the United States by the Constitution, nor prohibited by it to the States, are reserved to the States respectively, or to the people.

## The Bill of Rights End-Amendments To The Constitution Continue

### Amendment XI (1795)

The Judicial power of the United States shall nor be construed to extend to any suit in law or equity, commenced or prosecuted against one of the United States by Citizens of another State, or by Citizens or subjects of any foreign State.

### Amendment XII (1804)

The Electors shall meet in their respective states and vote by ballot for President and Vice President, one of whom, at least, shall not be an inhabitant of the same state with themselves; they shall name in their ballots the person voted for as President, and in distinct ballots the person voted for as Vice President, and they shall make distinct lists of all persons voted for as President and of all persons voted for as Vice President, and of the number of votes for each, which lists they shall sign and certify, and transmit sealed to the seat of the government of the United States, directed to the President of the Senate;—The President of the Senate shall, in the presence of Senate and House of Representatives, open all the certificates and the Votes shall then be counted;—The person having the greatest number of votes for President, shall be the President, if such number be a majority of the whole number of Electors appointed; and if no person have such majority, then from the persons having the highest numbers not exceeding three on the list of those voted for as President, the House of Representatives shall choose immediately, by ballot, the President. But in choosing the President, the votes shall be taken by states, the representation from each state having one vote; a quorum for this purpose shall consist of a member or members from two-thirds of the states, and a majority of all the staff shall be necessary to a choice. And if the House of Representatives shall not choose a President whenever the right of choice shall devolve upon them, before he fourth day of March next following,* then the Vice President shall act as President, as in the case of the death or other constitutional disability of the President.—The person having the greatest number of Votes as Vice President shall be the Vice President, if such number be a majority of the whole number of Electors appointed, and if no person have a majority, then from the two highest numbers on the list, the Senate shall choose the Vice President; a quorum for the purpose shall consist of two-thirds  of the whole number of Senators, and a majority of the whole number shall be necessary to a choice. But no person constitutionally ineligible to the office of President shall be eligible to that of Vice President of the United States.

### Amendment XIII (1865)

**Section 1** • Neither slavery nor involuntary servitude, except as a punishment for crime whereof the party shall have been duly convicted, shall exist within the United States, or any place subject to their jurisdiction.
Congress shall have the power to enforce this article by appropriate legislation.

### Amendment XIV (1868)

**Section 1** • All persons born or naturalized in the United States. and subject to the jurisdiction thereof, are citizens of the United States and of the State wherein they reside. No State shall make or enforce any law which shall abridge the privileges or immunities of citizens of the United States; nor shall any State deprive any person of life, liberty, or property, without due process of law; nor deny to any person within its jurisdiction the equal protect of the laws.
**Section 2** • Representatives shall be appointed among the several States according to their respective numbers, counting the whole number of persons in each State, excluding Indians not taxed. But when the right to vote at any election for the choice of electors for President and Vice President of the United States, Representatives in Congress, the Executive and Judicial officers of a State, or the members of the Legislature thereof, is denied to any of the male inhabitants of such State, being twenty-one years of age, and citizens of the United States, or in any way abridged, except for participation in rebellion, or other crime, the basis of representation therein shall be reduced in the proportion which the number of such male citizens shall bear to the whole number of male citizens twenty-one years of age in such State.
**Section 3** • No person shall be a Senator or Representative in Congress, or elector of President and Vice President, or hold any office, civil or military, under the United States, or under any State, who, having previously taken an oath, as a member of Congress, or as an officer of the United States, or as a member of any State legislature, or as an executive or judicial officer of any State, to support the Constitution of the United States, shall have engaged in insurrection or rebellion against the same, or given aid or comfort to the enemies thereof. But Congress may be a vote of two thirds of each House, remove such disability.
**Section 4** • The validity of the public debt of the United States, authorized by law, including debts incurred for payment of pensions and bounties for services in  suppressing insurrection or rebellion, shall not be questioned. But neither the United States nor any State shall assume or pay any debt or obligation incurred in aid of insurrection or rebellion against the United States, or any claim for the loss or emancipation of any slave; but all such debts, obligations, and claims shall be held illegal and void.
**Section 5** • The Congress shall have power to enforce, by appropriate legislation, the provisions of this article.

* Revised by the Twentieth Amendment.

### Amendment XV (1870)

Section 1 •  The right of citizens of the United States to vote shall not be denied or abridged by the United States or by any State on account of race, color, or previous conditions of servitude.
Section 2 •  The Congress shall have power to enforce this article by appropriate legislation.

### Amendment XVI (1913)

The Congress shall have power to lay and collect taxes on incomes, from whatever source derived, without apportionment among the several States, and without regard to any census or enumeration. [See comments on the 16th Admendment a separate attachemnt or enclosure]

### Amendment XVII (1913)

The Senate of the United States shall be composed of two Senators from each State, elected by the people thereof, for six years; and each Senator shall have one vote. The electors in each State shall have the qualifications requisite for electors of the most numerous branch of the State legislature.

When vacancies happen in the representation of any State in the Senate, the executive authority of such State shall issue writs of election to fill such vacancies: Provided, That the legislature of any State may empower the executive thereof to make temporary appointments until the people fill the vacancies by election as the legislature may direct.

This amendment shall not be so construed as to affect the election or term of any Senator chosen before it becomes valid as part of the Constitution.

### Amendment XVIII (1919)

Section 1 •  After one year from the ratification of this article the manufacture, sale, or transportation of intoxicating liquors within, the importation thereof into, or the exportation thereof from the United States and all territory subject to the jurisdiction thereof for beverage purposes is hereby prohibited.
Section 2 •  The Congress and the several States shall have concurrent power to enforce this article by appropriate legislation.
Section 3 •  This article shall be inoperative unless it shall have been ratified as an amendment to the Constitution by the legislatures of the several States, as provided in the Constitution within seven years from the date of the submission hereof to the States by the Congress.*

### Amendment XIX (1920)

The right of citizens of the United States to vote shall not be denied or abridged by the United States or by any State on account of sex.
Congress shall have power to enforce this article by appropriate legislation.

### Amendment XX (1933)

Section 1 •  The terms of the President and Vice President shall end at noon on the 20th day of January, and the terms of Senators and Representatives at noon on the 3rd day of January, of the years in which such terms would have ended if this article had not been ratified; and the terms of their successors shall then begin.
Section 2 •  The Congress shall assemble at least once in every year, and such meeting shall begin at noon on the 3rd day of January, unless they shall by law appoint a different day.

---

*Repealed by the Twenty-first Amendment.

Section 3 ⦁ If, at the time fixed for the eginning of the term of the President, the President elect shall have died, the Vice President elect shall become President. If a President shall not have been chosen before the time fixed for the beginning of his term, or if the President elect shall have failed to qualify, then the Vice President elect shall act as President until a President shall have qualified; and the Congress may by law provide for the case wherein neither a President elect nor a Vice President elect shall have qualified, declaring who shall then act as President, or the manner in which one who is to act shall be selected, and such person shall act accordingly until a President or Vice President shall have qualified.

Section 4 ⦁ The Congress may by law provide for the case of the death of any of the persons from whom the House of Representatives may choose a President whenever the right of choice shall have devolved upon them, and for the case of the death of any of the persons from whom the Senate may choose a Vice President whenever the right of choice shall have devolved upon them.

Section 5 ⦁ Sections 1 and 2 shall take effect on the 15th day of October following the ratification of this article.

Section 6 ⦁ This article shall be inoperative unless it shall have been ratified as an amendment to the Constitution by the legislatures of three-fourths of the several States within seven years from the date of its submission.

## Amendment XXI (1933)

Section 1 ⦁ The eighteenth article of amendment to the Constitution of the United States is hereby repealed.

Section 2 ⦁ The transportation or importation into any State, Territory, or possession of the United States for delivery or use therein of intoxicating liquors, in violation of the laws thereof, is hereby prohibited.

Section 3 ⦁ This article shall be inoperative unless it shall have been ratified as an amendment to the Constitution by conventions in the several States, as provided in the Constitution, within seven years from the date of the submission hereof to the States by the Congress.

## Amendment XXII (1951)

Section 1 ⦁ No person shall be elected to the office of the President more than twice, and no person who has held the office of President, or acted as President, for more than two years of a term to which some other person was elected President shall be elected to the office of President more than once. But this Article shall not apply to any person holding the office of President when this Article was proposed by the Congress, and shall not prevent any person who may be holding the office of President, or acting as President, during the term within which this Article becomes operative from holding the office of President or acting as President during the remainder of such term.

Section 2 ⦁ This article shall be inoperative unless it shall have been ratified as an amendment to the Constitution by the legislatures of three-fourths of the several States within seven years from the date of its submission to the States by the Congress.

## Amendment XXIII (1961)

Section 1 ⦁ The District constituting the seat of Government of the United States shall appoint in such manner as the Congress may direct:

A number of electors of President and Vice President equal to the whole number of Senators and Representatives in Congress to which the District would be entitled if it were a State, but in no event more than the least populous State; they shall be in addition to those appointed by the States, but they shall be considered, for the purposes of the election of President and Vice President, to be electors appointed by a State; and they shall meet in the District and perform such duties as provided by the twelfth article of amendment.

Section 2 ⦁ The Congress shall have power to enforce this article by appropriate legislation.

### Amendment XXIV (1964)

Section 1 • The right of citizens of the United States to vote in any primary or other election for President or Vice President, for electors for President or Vice President, or for Senator or Representative in Congress, shall not be denied or abridged by the United States or any state by reason of failure to pay any poll tax or other tax.

Section 2 • The Congress shall have the power to enforce this article by appropriate legislation.

### Amendment XXV (1967)

Section 1 • In case of the removal of the President from office or of his death or resignation, the Vice President shall become President.

Section 2 • Whenever there is a vacancy in the office of the Vice President, the President shall nominate a Vice President who shall take office upon confirmation by a majority vote of both Houses of Congress.

Section 3 • Whenever the President transmits to the President pro tempore of the Senate and the Speaker of the House of Representatives his written declaration that he is unable to discharge the powers and duties of his office, and until he transmits to them a written declaration to the contrary, such powers and duties shall be discharged by the Vice President as Aging President.

Section 4 • Whenever the Vice President and a majority of either the principal officers of the executive departments or of such other body as Congress may by law provide, transmit to the President pro tempore of the Senate and the Speaker of the House of Representatives their written declaration that the President is unable to discharge the powers and duties of his office, the Vice President shall immediately assume the powers and duties of the office as Acting President.

Thereafter, when the President transmits to the President pro tempore of the Senate and the Speaker of the House of Representatives his written declaration that no inability exists, he shall resume the powers and duties of his office unless the Vice President and a majority of either the principal officers of the executive departments or of such other body as Congress may by law provide, transmit within four days to the President pro tempore of the Senate and the Speaker of the House of Representatives their written declaration that the President is unable to discharge the powers and duties of his office. Thereupon Congress shall decide the issue, assembling within forty-eight hours for that purpose if not in session. If the Congress, within twenty-one days after receipt of the latter written declaration or, if Congress is not in session, within twenty-one days after Congress is required to assemble, determines by two-thirds vote of both Houses that the President is unable to discharge the powers and duties of his office, the Vice President shall continue to discharge the same as Acting President; otherwise, the President shall resume the powers and duties of his office.

### Amendment XXVI (1971)

Section 1 • The right of citizens of the United States, who are eighteen years of age or older, to vote shall not be denied or abridged by the United States or any state on account of age.

Section 2 • The Congress shall have the power to enforce this article by appropriate legislation.

## What the IRS Does Not Want You to Know About Supreme Court Rulings Regarding The 16th Amendment

The 16th Amendment was applicable only to indirect excise taxes on privileges and revenue taxable activities.

The first supreme Court case to challenge the erroneous idea that the 16th Amendment change the Constitution and allowed direct taxes to be issued without apportionment, was the Brushaber v. Union Pacific RR, (1916).

Following are excerpts from this historic decision: "The confusion ( Brushaber). . .arises from the conclusion that the Sixteenth Amendment provides for a hitherto unknown power of taxation, that is, a power to levy an income tax, which although direct, should not be subject to the regulation of apportionment...The far-reaching effect of Brushaber's erroneous assumption...if acceded to, would cause one provision of the Constitution to destroy another; that is , it would result in bringing the provisions of the Amendment exempting a direct tax from apportionment into irreconcilable conflict with the general requirement that all direct taxes must be apportioned ...This result, instead of simplifying the situation and making clear the limitation on the taxing power, which obviously the Amendment must have been intended to  accomplish, would create radical and destructive changes in our constitution system and multiply confusion... Indeed,  from any other view point, the Amendment demonstrates that no such purpose was intended and, on the contrary, shows that it was drawn with the objective of maintaining the limitations of the Constitution and harmonizing their operations...The 16th Amendment contains nothing repudiating of challenging the ruling of the Pollock Case...The 16th Amendment, as correctly interpreted, was limited to indirect taxes, and for that reasons is constitutional." Brushaber v. Union Pacific RR, 240 U. S. 1, at 10, 11, 12, 19

"The contention that the [16th] Amendment treats a tax on income as a  direct tax is...wholly without foundation." Brushaber, supra, at page 18

There is a vast misconception within America, fraudulently perpetuated by the IRS, that the 16th Amendment authorized Congress to impose a direct, non-apportioned individual income Tax on the compensation for labor earned by citizens, living and working in the 50 states. This is not true! It was determined by the supreme Court, that the 16th Amendment did NOT change the Constitution because the apportionment clauses were never repealed or altered.  It is well settled in fact of Law that:

The 16th Amendment Did NOT give Congress any  new taxing authority that it did not have prior to the 16th Amendment (When  non-apportioned direct taxes on property were fond by the Supreme Court to be unconstitutional.)

"The Sixteenth Amendment must be construed in connection with the taxing clauses of the original Constitution and the effect attributed to them before the Amendment as adopted." Eisner v. Macomber, 252 U. S. 189, at 205 (1920)

"The 16th Amendment does not extend the power of taxation to new or excepted subjects...Neither can the tax be sustained on the person, measured by income. Such a tax would be by nature, a **capitation**' rather than an excise." Peck v. Lowe, 247 US 165

* Capitation Tax:  "A tax imposed upon a person at a fixed rate, regardless of the taxpayer' s ability to pay, Occupation, assets, or income." The Law Dictionary

"The 16th Amendment conferred no new power of taxation but simply prohibited the income tax from be taken out of the category of indirect taxation to which it inherently belongs..." Stanton v. Baltic Mining C., 240 US 103

As recently as 1979, Howard Zaritsky, a legislative attorney for the Congressional Research Service, for the Library of Congress, in responding to a request by Congress for a report on the applicability of the 16th Amendment, determined that "the 16th Amendment had No Legal Effect." The Zaritsky Report stated, "In 1916 the supreme Court [Brushaber] rendered its decision regarding the amendment. In essence the court stated that, there is no need for the 16th Amendment..."

"How little do my countrymen know what precious blessing they are in possession of and which no other people on Earth enjoy" Thomas Jefferson.

# YH WH led The Real King Charles' path through the Christ-

## Please Check out Gifted Records

These inspirational albums are loaded with great music for your mind, body and soul. Just type in one of the two choices below on SoundCloud to listen to snippets of the amazing songs. The albums can be purchased on Amazon, Spotify, Apple Music and iTunes.

1. "Celebrate Christmas with Friends and King Charles" by Gifted Records

2. "It's a Beautiful Day" by Gifted Records

**The Real King Charles is the writer of this Powerful Manual and the writer of 90% of the songs, and he is the owner of Gifted Records. Richard Walker is the cowriter of some of the songs on <u>It's a Beautiful Day</u> and is the main vocalist on both albums. He is also a good friend.**

# ABOUT THE AUTHOR

The Real King Charles is writing his bio with utmost respect for the Creator and the true rules of law. Before I was fully created and discharged from my mother's womb, there was an assassination attempt on my life. In biblical stories they always try to assassinate the baby after the baby was born. The evil forces tried to assassinate me before I was discharge from my mother womb.

America is the people's Promise Land. The Declaration of Independence States "That whenever any Form of Government becomes destructive of these ends, it is the Right of the People to alter or abolish it, and to institute new Government, laying its foundation on such principles and organizing its powers in such form, as to them shall seem most likely to effect their Safety and Happiness." I always felt different: I am a songwriter, an executive producer, an inventor, I was a professional boxer, telephone installer, I took up plumbing for three years in high school and I love constitutional law. I am now the author of most powerful Manual on the Planet, THE ONLY WAY OUT.

www.ingramcontent.com/pod-product-compliance
Lightning Source LLC
Chambersburg PA
CBHW052052190326
41519CB00002BA/198

*9780692169285*